Praise for *Moving*

"Glazer and Wool make the persuasive case that relationships will matter most in the future of marketing. *Moving to Outcomes* is a proven playbook for the next great opportunity in marketing: partnerships at scale."

—Keith Ferrazzi, #1 *New York Times* bestselling author and founder/chairman of Ferrazzi Greenlight and Go Forward to Work

"Global marketing partnerships have been driving growth for businesses of all sizes and industries. With *Moving to Outcomes,* Glazer and Wool bring the enormous potential of partnerships to the executive suite and share why partnerships offer an opportunity every business needs to seize."

—Adam Ross, CEO of Awin

"Partnerships have already played a key role on both sides of our business—acquiring new consumers and launching new merchant partners—and *Moving to Outcomes* shares how scalable, tech-enhanced partnerships will become a foundational marketing strategy that the C-suite can't afford to overlook. Glazer and Wool share a playbook for success for both publishers and e-commerce brands alike for the future of partnership marketing."

—Amit Patel, CEO and president of Rakuten Americas

"Glazer has done it again—making timely and challenging topics oh-so-readable! He and Wool have taken a wildly complex and dynamic modern marketing ecosystem and broken it down into clear and concise frameworks and action-oriented, practical advice for anyone out there trying to build a consumer-facing business."

—Laura Joukovski, CEO of Global
Fashion Brands at TechStyle

"Effective digital marketing is about people and relationships. *Moving to Outcomes* is the playbook for helping you build effective, outcome-based relationships with leading marketing partners to drive better ROI for your business."

—Ben Kirshner, founder of Tinuiti

"There are a lot of snake-oil salesmen who promise businesses that investing in online advertising will drive unlimited growth with minimal risk. Bob Glazer adroitly exposes such myths, giving readers a road map to finding success with paid media while also identifying alternatives that can help you avoid over-reliance on Google and Facebook."

—David Rodnitzky, founder and CEO of 3Q Digital

"Acceleration Partners has helped hundreds of brands achieve sustainable, scalable ROI through trusted affiliate marketing partnerships. In *Moving to Outcomes,* Glazer and Wool share their winning formula with the world on how to pay for marketing that works. A must read for any CEO/CMO who wants to diversify their digital marketing."

—Hannah Wharrier, managing director, digital marketing division, of Clarion Events

"No matter what your business is, your marketing strategy today probably isn't suited for tomorrow. With *Moving to Outcomes,* Glazer and Wool share the marketing playbook they've helped the best e-commerce brands run for years. Learn how you can prepare your business for the future with a strategy built on outcome-based marketing partnerships that drive scalable ROI."

—John Jantsch, founder of Duct Tape Marketing and bestselling author of *Duct Tape Marketing* and *The Ultimate Marketing Engine*

"*Moving to Outcomes* is a perfect guide to help businesses pay for marketing that works! For executives who want to compete in the next era of marketing, Glazer and Wool's playbook shouldn't be missed."

—Brian Scudamore, founder and CEO of 1-800-GOT-JUNK? and O2E Brands and bestselling author of *WTF?! (Willing to Fail)*

"*Moving to Outcomes* powerfully highlights that the needs of the marketer have never been more aligned with what our category is capable of delivering. Brand marketing and performance marketing are converging quickly, driven by the fundamental change of the power shift from the brand to the consumer. The growth channels of paid social and paid search have reached the point of diminishing returns, and C-suite marketers are recognizing that their go-forward growth engine will be built on sustainable, profitable marketing partnerships."

—Matthew Gilbert, CEO of Partnerize

"Every smart marketer knows the power of partnership marketing. This excellent book takes you through a deep understanding and implementation."

—Allan Dib, founder of Successwise and author of *The 1-Page Marketing Plan*

MOVING to OUTCOMES

Why Partnerships Are the Future of Marketing

ROBERT GLAZER
& MATT WOOL

Sourcebooks, Simple Truths, and the colophon are registered trademarks of Sourcebooks.

Published by Simple Truths, an imprint of Sourcebooks
P.O. Box 4410, Naperville, Illinois 60567-4410
(630) 961-3900
sourcebooks.com

Cataloging-in-Publication Data is on file with the Library of Congress.

Printed and bound in the United States of America.
SB 10 9 8 7 6 5 4 3

Table of Contents

Glossary

OUTCOME: Something that follows as a result or consequence.

AFFILIATE MARKETING: A marketing model in which brands pay partners who drive certain results for their businesses. An affiliate can be any person or group that has an audience and potential influence over the desired outcome, whether that is a purchase, a lead, or another form of definitive action.

PARTNERSHIP MARKETING: Outcome-based marketing relationships enabled at scale through digital technology. Affiliate marketing is both a precursor to partnership marketing and is also now a subset.

PARTNER (AFFILIATE/PUBLISHER): An individual or business that showcases another brand's goods or services and receives a commission for each outcome it delivers.

BRAND (RETAILER, MERCHANT, ADVERTISER): For the purposes of this book, people who sell things are defined as brands, retailers, merchants, or advertisers. These terms are used interchangeably. Examples of brands include companies such as Walmart, Expedia, Uber, and Warby Parker.

Introduction

"What is a cynic? A man who knows the price
of everything and the value of nothing."

—OSCAR WILDE

In early 2000, a former *New York Magazine* writer named Dany
Levy found herself in a transitory period of unemployment as she
prepared to apply to business school. She began to spend hours
surfing the internet, still in its early stage, and realized that many
users were simply overwhelmed by the scale of the World Wide
Web. Like any good entrepreneur, Levy turned this problem—an
overwhelmingly vast internet landscape—into an opportunity.
She pulled seven hundred contacts from her personal Rolodex
and sent a newsletter in March 2000. It was called *DailyCandy*.

DailyCandy was defined by its simplicity and brevity. Each installment featured a single product, broadcast to a list of engaged, well-targeted subscribers—predominantly city-dwelling, professional young women. *DailyCandy* grew quickly to 285,000 subscribers by 2003 and to 1.2 million by 2008.[1]

Potential sponsors soon discovered that *DailyCandy* was a brand multiplier; a mention in the newsletter could help jump-start a product, even a company, to success. Several well-known brands, including the blow-dry salon Drybar and the clothing retailer Nasty Gal, benefited from an appearance in *DailyCandy*.

Soon, the word spread about the power of this newsletter, and brands targeting young, city-dwelling women competed to be featured. Levy was able to charge increasingly higher prices for advertising, because brands began to believe they had to get into *DailyCandy* at any cost necessary. They were willing to pay large up-front placement fees just to get featured.

Over time, however, the cost of advertising in *DailyCandy* became prohibitive for many brands. Brands that managed to get their products promoted in *DailyCandy* early in its existence benefited from being early adopters and took advantage of cost-effective advertising that drove meaningful results for their businesses. Those who learned about it at the height of its popularity paid hefty fees that did more for *DailyCandy*'s profit than their own businesses.

It wasn't that *DailyCandy* was either universally effective or ineffective for advertisers. Instead, there were two issues. First, *DailyCandy*'s high price made the newsletter cost prohibitive for many brands, pricing out a large number of prospective advertisers. Second, the high price became difficult for even large brands to justify without a commensurate return on investment (ROI). While brands were willing to take a risk and invest in *DailyCandy* up to a certain price point, the price eventually became too high for most brands.

DailyCandy's fall came quickly. Comcast purchased the company for $120 million in 2008 and then ultimately shut the newsletter down a few years after merging with NBCUniversal.

It's difficult for a channel to stay relevant when brands can no longer be confident that an investment will yield the desired outcome, and as a result of its success, *DailyCandy* priced itself out of the market. An all too familiar sequence of events was complete.

A Broken Cycle

The rise and fall of *DailyCandy* is emblematic of a dysfunctional cycle that most marketers will find familiar:

▶ A new marketing channel opens and gains significant

traction; a few early adopters who are willing to take a risk reap outsize rewards.

▶ As awareness of the channel expands, creating more potential exposure, the price of the channel escalates as well.

▶ Eventually, the channel becomes inefficiently expensive for all but the most sophisticated players and those willing to trade volume for margin, pushing many businesses to search for a new channel.

This cycle can make it feel as if marketing, especially digital marketing, has become a giant game of whack-a-mole.

The very largest brands, with billion-dollar marketing budgets, can often afford to hang around longer as a maturing channel's prices increase, even though their actual ROI might not justify the spend. The majority of brands, however, need exceptionally good timing to extract sustainable profit from many of these channels and cycles.

Here's the thing, though: this cycle applies to more than just the hot new marketing channel. Brands also eventually become frustrated with the ROI from investing with the Goliaths of the digital marketing world: Google, Facebook, and, to an increasing degree, Amazon (together, the "Triopoly"). Many businesses today are overly reliant on a concentrated set of marketing tactics such as paid social, paid search, and programmatic display, the fancy new term for digital banner ads. And each year, these standard digital tactics become less profitable as demand grows faster than supply in what is essentially a giant auction.

While this dynamic has been developing for many years, things are even more challenging now due to transformational shifts in the way we market, sell, and shop. Not only do marketers have to stay ahead of rapid changes pushed by the rise of brands with direct-to-consumer (DTC) business models, but they also have to simultaneously compete against e-commerce giants like Amazon for awareness and customers. And they have to do it in a world where changing attitudes toward privacy are making customer targeting increasingly more difficult.

The digital Goliaths of today aren't disappearing anytime soon and will continue to be key drivers of marketing for many companies. But any business, large or small, that fails to diversify their marketing portfolios beyond those dominant players will likely face decreased profitability and diminishing control over their marketing dollars.

Think about your marketing strategy as you would consider an investment portfolio. Every investment guru advises diversifying your stock market assets to protect against declines in some types of assets. Additionally, if you want better returns, you need to adjust your holdings through diversification and get outside the traditional asset classes. Once an asset class reaches maturity and ubiquity, you are much less likely to see above-average returns. Investors can't beat the market by investing in the biggest names of today; instead, they need to find the next Microsoft, Amazon, or Tesla.

Marketers today have a choice. They can keep doubling down on advertising with the digital Goliaths of today or begin to diversify and invest in other marketing channels, with an eye toward the future.

About This Book

This book is about one of these marketing channels—one that offers a superior and predictable ROI, a way to create a defensible competitive advantage, and effective diversification in the marketing portfolio. That channel is partnerships.

Partnership marketing is not new; it has existed in many different forms and under many different names, such as affiliate marketing, for decades. However, thanks to transformative changes in enabling technology and pricing models as well as a change in both supply and demand, partnership marketing now exists in a more automated, scalable form that few companies have fully leveraged to date.

Most important, however, is that partnership marketing has two distinct advantages over other digital marketing channels.

First, partnership marketing provides control and sustainability, because it uses a pricing model in which companies can determine their ideal profit margins, set their costs accordingly, and pay for marketing only after a desired event occurs, rather than leaving pricing to external parties. Second, because partnership marketing is relationship-based and not driven by impersonal bidding for placements, companies can build partnerships and programs over time that provide them with a strategic advantage over competitors. When scaled properly, partnership marketing offers the ability to make inroads against even much larger players such as Amazon in ways that are often not possible through other forms of performance-based marketing.

This book investigates these concepts in detail. We begin by exploring why many traditional digital marketing channels are rapidly losing efficacy for brands, why partnership marketing is uniquely positioned to help businesses of all sizes, and why partnership marketing offers improved ROI in response to recent shifts in how business is conducted. While several of these trends will be familiar, you may be surprised to see how they consistently point toward a clear direction: a prioritization of marketing channels and partnerships that allow companies to pay for outcomes, not inputs.

Then, we give a clear illustration of how partnership marketing works and share examples of the results it can generate. Most importantly, we explain how you can use it to create a competitive advantage for your business. Even if your company is already engaged in some aspect of partnership marketing, you will see how it can create more efficiency, transparency, and scale in many different facets of your brand's marketing, including partnerships, influencer marketing, and business development.

As Warren Buffett once said, "What the wise do in the beginning, fools do in the end." The biggest dividends of the partnership marketing revolution will go to the marketers who get in early and establish successful programs before their competitors can catch up. This is not a channel where brands can simply arrive late, bid high, and be rewarded. You can reap the benefits of partnership marketing by laying the foundation for your program now, before your competitors get in the game.

You don't have to abandon your other digital marketing initiatives, but once you discover how efficient and effective partnership marketing can be, it's easy to imagine that the model will become a crucial part of your modern marketing portfolio.

1.

The Case for Partnerships

> "Alone we can do so little;
> together we can do so much."
>
> —HELEN KELLER

To illustrate the effectiveness of partnership marketing, let's start with a simple question. Would you rather:

A: Pay $100 for an ad placement that yields 1000 advertising impressions but leads to only five sales?

B: Offer a marketing partner $10 per completed sale, leading to ten sales for $100 each?

You don't need an MBA to know you should choose B. It's a marketer's dream to invest their budget in a channel where the outcomes are set in advance and payment comes due only after those outcomes are delivered.

This is the crucial advantage that partnership marketing has over similar data-driven models under the umbrella of performance-based marketing. With many forms of performance-based marketing (a catchall phrase that now encompasses most forms of digital marketing), you can measure the effectiveness of your advertisement only by analyzing campaign data retroactively, rather than paying for only the outcomes you seek. This structure allows you to make small adjustments and smarter decisions in the future, but you still end up paying for poor results if a campaign underperforms. Brands don't have any guarantees in many channels of performance-based marketing—they can only learn from their mistakes.

In contrast, in partnership marketing, you only have to pay for what works, based on your definition of success. Rather than investing up front and hoping for the best, you pay an agreed-upon percentage or fee, billed only after you've secured the desired outcome, be it revenue, leads, customers, or some other result. And because partners get paid according to those same metrics, it is in their best interests to deliver the right outcomes. The incentives of brands and partners are aligned.

Partnership marketing is highly effective. Under the correct conditions and when managed properly, it offers three key differentiating advantages.

First, partnership marketing is **profitable**—by definition. Companies only pay partners a percentage of each sale or qualified lead, so a company can set their pricing up front to ensure their profit margin goals are met in the channel.

Second, partnership marketing is **scalable**, in terms of both investment and technology. A company can use a partnership marketing platform to manage hundreds or thousands of marketing partnerships easily, allowing brands to build their partnership programs in a scalable, trackable way, all while reducing the administrative burden. Partnership marketing also maintains efficiency as it scales—if you love paying 10 percent for $10 of revenue, the same should be true of paying 10 percent for $1,000 of revenue.

And to return to the earlier investing analogy, by working across a large number of partners rather than relying heavily on a few, advertisers can diversify and reduce risk. Partners in your program engage potential customers in different ways and with different strategies, offering built-in diversification. For example, if one partner or partner type starts to struggle, there are many others using completely different tactics and reaching different audience sets who will continue to perform well.

3

Finally, partnership marketing is **sustainable**. Brands do not have to repeatedly bid more to maintain their advantage, and partners have reasons to stay and double down with the brands who treat them well and pay them fairly. This creates a sense of mutual loyalty. This is far better than being at the mercy of digital slot machines whose prices keep rising or constantly chasing the "it" channel of the moment that will almost certainly either become too expensive, like *DailyCandy*, or become a less relevant platform when they lose a large percentage of their audience to the next new thing.

With a comprehensive partnership marketing program, companies can bring all sorts of partnership-driven marketing initiatives onto a single technology platform that automates partner onboarding, tracking, and payment in a fully transparent way. Brands can create a single program that includes affiliate marketing, influencer marketing, ambassador marketing, brand-to-brand partnerships, and even certain aspects of business development and client-referral programs. Plus, they can manage all these partners in a truly relationship-oriented way. Many of today's current marketing and sales channels can be enhanced with a partnership framework, where all involved parties are incentivized to deliver certain outcomes that the brand wants most.

The difference between partnership marketing and traditional marketing channels becomes clear when closely examined.

Many aspects of traditional digital marketing can feel like putting on a blindfold and playing a high-stakes game of darts, whereas partnership marketing involves finding a partner who can hit the dartboard for you and who asks for their cut of the prize money only after they help you win. Brands can exchange guesswork for verifiable results, and marketing partners are incentivized to deliver those results.

Partnership marketing also enables brands to skip to the bottom of the marketing funnel, ignoring the noise and distractions at the top. To illustrate this, consider an offline business example. Imagine that the owner of a boat rental shop decides to incentivize the local resort concierge for referrals. If the boat rental shop offers the concierge a small fee—say, $10—for every prospective customer they send over, the concierge will try to send every guest who stops by their desk, regardless of how interested the guest is in renting a boat.

In contrast, let's say the rental shop owner offers a higher success fee—say, 10 percent of all bookings—as a commission for each sale the concierge generates. The concierge will likely be far more discerning when referring guests to the rental shop. They'll ask the right questions and send only the most qualified possible leads, as the concierge gets paid only if their referrals actually rent. The concierge gets paid more per qualified lead, the shop gets fewer (but better qualified) referrals and pays only for confirmed customers, and everyone is better off.

This example demonstrates how partnership marketing better directs potential customers to the bottom of the marketing funnel. This model puts the focus on the right objectives and incentives—sales, leads, or other tangible outcomes. It also gives the partners the data they need to help identify which referrals ultimately generated a conversion so the partners can alter their approach going forward. Plus, this model ensures that the right brands are connected to the right publishers, rather than creating a scenario where an ad for beachwear appears on a site selling arctic vacation packages.

But the most crucial advantage of partnership marketing may be the way it creates an alignment of incentives.

In a partnership marketing relationship, partners and advertisers agree on the desired outcome in advance and set commissions based on the achievement of that outcome. In other words, the partner's incentive aligns with what the advertiser wants most. As University of Chicago economist Eric Budish explained, "Where there's a revenue split, that makes both sides want to grow the pie. The idea that, out of every dollar, I get 80 cents, you get 20 cents, and that aligns our incentives—that's just good old-fashioned economics."[1]

So if partnership marketing is so great, why do we need

to write a book to explain its virtues? Shouldn't it be ubiquitous already and a go-to channel for chief marketing officers (CMOs)?

In reality, the model is popular—the partnership management platform Partnerize found that 74 percent of companies consider partnerships and affiliate marketing campaigns to be high priorities for their businesses.[2] But partnership marketing is lagging in awareness and understanding for three main reasons.

▶ It simply lacks the same branding and anchor tenants of other digital marketing channels. There isn't yet a Google, Facebook, or Amazon of partnership marketing that every person knows; the industry is far more fractured, which is both a challenge and a benefit.

▶ Partnership marketing is not a product that can be sold in the same way as other digital marketing channels, in which large sales teams from platforms consistently push for higher spending levels. In fact, the market works the other way: brands recruit their partners and bring them into a campaign.

▶ Partnership marketing programs are developed much more organically over time; you can't buy volume in the same way and turn it up and down on a dime as you can with paid search and social. This means that it doesn't have the same splashy effect on a CMO's reporting as a big Facebook campaign.

While partnership marketing needs better PR, it has worked reliably for many years under several names and variations. In fact, some brands have become highly successful running this type of marketing program without even knowing its name.

The Accidental Partnership Program

In 2015, Mike Salguero was making a significant shift in his diet. His wife, Karlene, was diagnosed with a thyroid condition, and they were attempting to follow an anti-inflammatory diet that prioritized grass-fed meat. Unable to find much of it in their local stores, Salguero found himself purchasing large quantities of beef from a local farmer, buying garbage bags full of meat in parking lot transactions. Salguero realized how convenient it would be to have grass-fed, well-sourced meat delivered to his home and saw the potential for a business. He started one himself, a DTC meat company called ButcherBox.[3]

I met Salguero when we were both members of the Boston chapter of Entrepreneurs Organization (EO Boston), a peer-to-peer member association for entrepreneurial business owners. When I caught up with him shortly after he launched

ButcherBox, we chatted about how affiliate marketing could work for his business. But with $10,000 to $20,000 in monthly recurring revenue, ButcherBox was far smaller than Acceleration Partners' typical affiliate management client, so we didn't bring them on board at the time.

Barely two years after that conversation, Salguero received EO Boston's Member of the Year Award. At the awards dinner, we learned that ButcherBox's revenue had grown to over $2 million per month, without any outside capital.[4] When I asked Salguero how he had scaled so quickly, I realized that he had inadvertently built a next-generation partnership marketing program without realizing how much he'd emulated the model.

ButcherBox sought out several of the most influential people in their industry, contacting top paleo-diet blogs, nutrition sites, fitness coaches, and other publishers who had credibility and a sizeable audience of health-passionate followers. Rather than paying up front for sponsorships, ButcherBox offered to track the success of each partnership through software and pay a larger success fee, showing partners how they would make more money with this model. In some cases, they also guaranteed the partner a minimum fee to share some of the up-front risk to get them going.

This one channel accounted for a majority of ButcherBox's sales from 2015 to 2017 while also generating significant brand awareness and word of mouth. In turn, the company invested progressively more money into these marketing partnerships, creating higher sales volume and generating exponentially more revenue.

By using a marketing model in which they paid only for successful customer acquisition, ButcherBox grew like a venture-backed company, without the need for outside capital. Their marketing expenses were paid after their revenue was secured, as partners are often paid thirty to sixty days after their sales are recorded, to account for returns and cancellations.

Today, ButcherBox is dramatically outperforming several venture-backed subscription services that spent all their money at the online marketing auction just to attract unprofitable and transactional customers. ButcherBox has had a meteoric rise that wasn't fueled by the traditional playbook of spending millions of investment dollars on customer acquisition.

This is the impact of partnership marketing executed well. Companies of all sizes can build marketing partnerships that create scalable revenue without the potential pitfalls of auction-style and up-front pricing models that many popular digital marketing channels have. Partnership marketing is an ideal way to grow profitably, maintain strong cash flow, and minimize marketing risk. Partnership marketing was transformative for ButcherBox and is becoming a key part of the growth playbook for countless other businesses as well.

Despite the many success stories like ButcherBox's, there are still many brands that do not see partnership marketing as a key tool in a CMO's toolbox, and they are spending the majority of their budgets with the digital Goliaths. Why is this?

The answer is complicated. Many companies today have different forms of partner programs, where they manage, track, and pay each partner on a manual basis, with a bunch of disconnected tools and processes, including spreadsheets. However, very few companies have figured out how to bring it all together under one roof and leverage the model to its full potential. Understanding why requires some historical context.

A Quick Trip Down Memory Lane

It's time for a short review of the early days of digital marketing.

Since the advent of the printing press, marketing has been entirely input driven—companies were most focused on getting placements in the most prominent media of the day. These were analog media such as magazines, billboards, and television ads. However, as previously discussed, it was difficult to know with any degree of certainty how effective these ads were. Many marketers found themselves in the same situation the merchant and marketing pioneer John Wanamaker faced more than one hundred years ago when he famously said, "Half my advertising spend is wasted; the trouble is, I don't know which half."

While brands could estimate how many people drove by a billboard each day or read a certain newspaper, there was no reliable way to measure how many people saw an ad, let alone purchased the product as a result of it. Brands paid for the potential exposure and attempted to make an educated guess about the sales, leads, or conversions their advertising actually created.

As the internet took off in the mid-1990s, digital advertising inventory was initially sold in the same way, priced according to the number of user impressions (views) or the number of banner advertisements placed. This model was referred to as CPM, or cost per thousand impressions. This technology-enabled channel was not much of an improvement on the billboard model; the ads were essentially just digital billboards. You paid for the potential—the number of people who *might* see your advertisement—without any guaranteed sales or traffic.

The first significant change in digital advertising arrived in 1998, when Goto.com began offering advertisements that charged per click. Google soon followed with their own version called Google AdWords, and the pay-per-click (PPC) channel was born. Today, paid search is a massive market globally, with GoogleAds alone generating $147 billion in revenue in 2020.[5]

While clicks weren't a perfect metric, they formed a better

link between advertising dollars and the traffic produced by those ads than anything that existed before. For the first time, PPC made it possible to know and pay for how many people visited your site rather than saw the advertisement. This metric was particularly relevant for the first generation of DTC brands that sold to customers only through their own websites and as a result saw online marketing as an acquisition channel rather than just a branding exercise.

It was around this same time that the first marketing model that allowed brands to pay for their desired outcomes arrived: affiliate marketing.

Affiliate marketing began in the late 1990s, with Amazon being credited as the first major company to launch an affiliate program, Amazon Associates, which endures today with an estimated one million partners globally. Early affiliate marketing was the first framework that gave companies a scalable way to pay marketing partners a commission based on the actual sales generated for a given product or service. Specifically, it leveraged digital technology to track a user from a click on a publisher or affiliate website all the way through to purchase on the brand's website. Affiliate marketing was the earliest model that allowed brands to pay for outcomes rather than inputs such as clicks or impressions.

Other companies soon followed suit, developing tracking

technology as a third-party solution available for license. These businesses then served as facilitators connecting thousands of brands—called advertisers or merchants—with website publishers who wanted to serve as affiliates on a cost-per-action (CPA) basis. This technology led to the creation of several major affiliate networks, such as BeFree, Commission Junction (now CJ Affiliate), and LinkShare (now Rakuten Marketing). Brands hosted their programs on one or more of these networks, and the networks recruited, tracked, and paid publishers, taking a percentage of the sale or the commission paid as a performance fee. This affiliate network technology was the glue that held it all together, enabling these sorts of partnerships at scale for the first time.

While affiliate marketing was highly successful, the first generation of the model was also marked by some questionable practices. Most notably, there were inherent conflicts of interest in a model where affiliate networks represented both publishers and advertisers in the same transaction, often leading to lax oversight and misaligned incentives in those early days.

Affiliate marketing at that time was also very transactional and lacked transparency. The relatively limited regulations and protections for brands led to several instances of significant fraud that cast the industry in a poor light for years to come. In fact, many of the marketing leaders during those days went on to avoid the channel in subsequent roles due to their negative experiences during this era.

The problems with affiliate marketing in the early years were less about the model itself and had more to do with poor oversight stemming from conflicts of interest posed by the dual representation, overreliance on a last-click attribution model, and a business model that stood essentially unchallenged for more than two decades (which we will talk about in more detail in chapter 6). However, the early model laid the foundation for the reemergence of partnership marketing today in a more reputable and effective form.

Partnership Marketing Takes the Stage

Affiliate marketing laid the groundwork for the partnership marketing model described earlier in this chapter. People often ask us if it's a precursor to partnership marketing or a subset of it; the answer is that it's both. Partnership marketing features the same outcome-based payment structure as affiliate marketing but with better technology, increased brand control, many new types of partners, and a focus on a high quality and volume of revenue.

Though both models use the same outcome-based payment structure, there is a key distinction between affiliate marketing and partnership marketing. Affiliate marketing is essentially one slice of the emerging and much bigger partnership marketing pie.

Partnership marketing is built upon affiliate marketing principles but has evolved from it in a few key ways, leveraging technological improvements and new possibilities in tracking, reporting, and commissioning. To outline these improvements specifically, we'll draw from our previous book, *Performance Partnerships*, which outlined how a high-quality partnership marketing program has four key components:

1. **A CPA framework:** Just like affiliate marketing, partnership marketing programs require brands to pay only for the outcomes their marketing partners deliver. The desired outcome is set by each brand and agreed upon in advance so that there is no ambiguity about what needs to be delivered. CPA can be set up as a commission on each sale delivered, a small fee for each lead generated, or a payment when a certain volume of web traffic is driven to a brand's site. The outcome varies, but the principle does not—as we say throughout this book, in partnership marketing, you pay only for what you get, not for what's promised to you. While some partners have fixed fee placements as part of their compensation, CPA is the dominant payment model in partnership marketing.

2. **Transparency:** This is where we historically start to see a divergence between affiliate marketing and partnership marketing. While some affiliates are highly transparent and communicative about their tactics, that is not a guaranteed element in a traditional affiliate program. In the past, some larger affiliates, who had the clout to set their own terms when working with brands, refused to disclose their tactics. While they claimed this was to protect proprietary methods and information, it also opened the possibility for fraud and made brands uneasy about those relationships.

   Partnership marketing does not allow this type of opacity. With a partnership marketing program, brands insist on working with partners who are transparent about what they're doing, what their results are, and how the brands are being represented.

3. **A real, trusting relationship:** Traditional affiliate marketing often had a high degree of anonymity, with many brands not entirely aware of the identity or tactics of some of their most lucrative publishers, as noted earlier. This distance is especially evident if brands are working with an opaque network that does not disclose the identity of its publishers. In contrast, a partnership marketing program implies an active ongoing relationship between the brand and the partner.

This degree of relationship management also helps align the long-term incentives between the partner and the brand— with each party less focused on each individual transaction. This loyalty in turn makes a partnership marketing program more sustainable over time for both the partner and the brand.

4. **Real-time tracking and payment:** An indispensable part of a partnership marketing platform is a software solution that tracks all actions and outcomes produced by a partner, verifies those results, pays commissions and performance fees, and provides consistent real-time reporting to both brands and partners. While in the past, this type of tracking and payment for traditional affiliate partners was managed through third-party networks, brands can now use software-as-a-service (SaaS) platforms to achieve the same functionality with all types of partners.

Partnership marketing offers much more relationship building, sustainability, and incentive alignment than brands can get marketing through the most popular digital channels. As you will see in the next chapters, when it comes to marketing exclusively and successfully through some of the largest digital channels today, we may be closer to the ninth inning of the ball game than the beginning. Businesses are earning progressively smaller ROIs for the same dollar of investment.

While you haven't yet missed the boat on partnership marketing, your time to get ahead in the channel and beat the rush to the exits for some of the popular channels showing increasingly diminished returns may be limited. We hope to share the playbook to make this timely shift.

Key Takeaways

▶ Partnership marketing is a profitable, scalable, sustainable channel brands can use to grow their businesses.

▶ Partnership marketing creates an incentive alignment between brands and partners to drive mutually beneficial, agreed-upon outcomes.

▶ Partnership marketing is built on a CPA (cost-per-action) framework; transparency; real, trusting relationships; and real-time tracking and payment.

Up Next

How changes to the way we buy, sell, and market products creates the ideal environment for partnership marketing.

2.

What Has Changed

"Time changes everything except
something within us which is
always surprised by change."
—THOMAS HARDY

In addition to the aforementioned shifting incentives and the technological changes that have made partnership marketing more attractive for companies, it's also worth exploring how the way we market, sell, and even shop has changed drastically in recent years and why partnership marketing is an excellent option for the commercial world of today and tomorrow.

In 2019, one of the most popular products in modern consumer history turned sixty years old—Mattel's iconic Barbie doll. Barbie has been one of the world's most reliable retail brands, charming customers across generations, personifying more than two hundred careers, imitating celebrities from Audrey Hepburn to J. K. Rowling, and even earning a reputation as a poor role model for young girls.[1]

Even though times have changed and kids spend more time playing digitally rather than physically, Barbie endures. Mattel even enjoyed a surge of sales during the COVID-19 pandemic, as parents were desperate to occupy kids stuck at home during lockdown.[2]

Mattel made Barbie an iconic toy through their mastery of 1960s marketing practices. Knowing that parents weren't won over by Barbie's waif-thin model, they instead advertised the toy directly to children to create demand. While generating toy demand through child-targeted marketing seems to be an obvious tactic today, it wasn't at the time. In fact, Mattel invented this strategy in 1955, four years before the birth of Barbie, when they began sponsoring the popular children's television program *The Mickey Mouse Club*.

Mattel's Barbie campaigns demonstrated their mastery of that era of marketing. They knew advertising directly to children would create brand awareness for their product, even if parents wouldn't have been inclined to purchase the doll for their kids of their own volition. When kids constantly saw ads for Barbie, they wanted the doll and asked for it. Toy stores responded by making Barbie a centerpiece of their displays, and customers bought in droves. Mattel made money, stores made money, and kids still play with Barbie more than sixty years later.

Even though brands successfully replicated Mattel's Barbie strategy for decades, it does not align with the realities of the market today. The next four sections explain why.

The Old Customer Acquisition Cycle

Mattel's awareness-driven marketing strategy was a dominant approach in the commercial market of the 1960s. As most marketers know, the relationship between manufacturers, vendors, and customers looked very different than it does today. The customer acquisition cycle used to look like this:

1. A wholesale brand designs and makes a product.

2. The brand creates awareness and demand for the product, typically through PR and awareness-generating placements in top mediums such as television or newspapers.

3. The brand sells its products wholesale to stores; by this point, the brand's advertising has created enough demand for stores to want to invest in the product.

4. The brand manages fulfillment of all orders, ensuring that its products are successfully delivered to stores.

5. The brand conducts customer service with stores as needed.

Absent from this cycle are the customers who eventually buy the brand's product. Brands didn't interact with the end users of their products—a brand's job was to create a broad level of brand awareness, sell the product to vendors, and get the store shelves stocked.

It's easy to see why the final outcomes of marketing—sales to end users—weren't relevant or necessary in this value chain. Brands didn't need to tie their marketing to end-user sales because the goal of the marketing wasn't to convince individuals to buy their products. Instead, their advertising's primary goal was creating a buzz, or awareness, about their product that convinced vendors it was worthwhile to stock the product in their stores. Customer-facing marketing was the work of the vendors, not the wholesale brands that supplied their wares.

Even in the early days of e-commerce, this customer acquisition cycle continued to be the prevailing model. Though progressively more customers began shopping online, they were still mostly buying from online department stores rather than the brands themselves.

But as people got more comfortable buying online, it opened up a new opportunity for brands to reach their customers directly. A monumental shift in the momentum for the DTC model came in 2011, when an unknown upstart decided to take on an industry giant with a $3 box of razor blades.

The DTC Revolution

In 2011, a pair of entrepreneurs named Michael Dubin and Mark Levine challenged an industry ruled by a few giant companies. They did this by asking a question that changed business: Is Gillette *really* the best a man can get?

The pair were frustrated by the process of buying razors and blades in a store, where blades from giants like Gillette were priced so high that stores had to keep them in locked display cases. Betting that others were also looking for a cheap, convenient alternative, Dubin and Levine launched a company called Dollar Shave Club and began selling razors and blades for as cheap as $3 per month, shipping them directly to customers.

Dollar Shave Club claims to have received 12,000 signups within forty-eight hours of their launch, which was announced with a funny viral YouTube video with the slogan "Our blades are $&*# great."[3] Within a year of launching, they raised over a million dollars in seed money; within a decade, they had a $1 billion valuation, which is clear testament to the market's underestimation of their ability to disrupt the razor industry.

Dollar Shave Club was just one of many start-ups that upended the established norms of how we buy. In retrospect, it seems obvious that people would want a cheaper, more convenient way to buy razors. It wasn't long before other brands began having similar success selling products that once seemed impossible to sell outside a store—including personal items such as mattresses and eyeglasses.

The COVID-19 pandemic further accelerated our understanding of which products can be sold online without an in-person experience. We still don't know the limits of what customers are willing to buy virtually; it would have seemed outrageous ten years ago to buy a car online, but Carvana has recently broken through that seemingly impassible barrier as well.

If a company can offer a good product at a better price point, they can take their case directly to the consumer without spending millions to break into an established supply chain and distribution network. Companies that sell directly to their end users can also develop strong relationships with and gain better knowledge of them.

This great shift has prompted an explosion of a new vertical in business: the DTC brands. DTC businesses established a new customer acquisition cycle, one where they sell directly to users, fulfill orders, and manage customer relationships themselves.

Because DTC brands sell directly to customers, their primary objective with marketing is to directly generate new sales and customers. Sure, DTC companies want to build a brand, but the best way to do this is often to get their products into the hands of as many customers as possible, as soon as possible, and let those buyers talk about the products to their friends and networks.

All brands selling online increasingly want the bulk of their marketing budgets focused on acquiring customers, leads, or traffic. To that end, Statista found that the spend for affiliate marketing increased every year between 2010 and 2021, more than quadrupling in that span.[4] Paying for outcomes is understandably becoming more popular.

Digital technology has made it easier to track the acquisition of individual customers, so the logical next step is to align advertising dollars with those outcomes.

Subscription Addiction

In addition to disrupting the overpriced razor market, Dollar Shave Club pioneered another aspect of the DTC revolution: the rise of subscription services. The increased prevalence of this business model—in which brands aim for customers to subscribe to their product or service indefinitely—has, in turn, increased the value of partnership marketing.

The economics of subscription services can be clearly seen in media streaming. Rather than charging a flat rate for access to a constantly expanding selection of shows and movies, Netflix brings in revenue from the same customers each month, generating consistent profit. Because users can unsubscribe at any time, the buyers still maintain some control in the arrangement, even though these subscription deals are often a windfall for the companies that offer them.

Companies selling everything from personal hygiene products to meat to coffee often offer a subscription model to ensure that each sale they close can potentially create recurring value from that customer. These companies view each customer as a potential long-term relationship, not a one-time deal, and value them as such.

The subscription model has led to the popularization of the lifetime value (LTV) metric. Because e-commerce and DTC selling have made it so easy to turn customers into subscribers, many brands view customer acquisition in terms of LTV rather than as a single transaction. When brands view customer acquisition in this way, the acquisition value of a new customer, especially a subscriber, grows.

The result is that brands are willing to pay a premium to acquire the right kind of customers. And partnership marketing is uniquely set up to deliver those types of loyal, long-term consumers.

Blending Content and Commerce

In this new world of DTC brands, the shift from in-store to online shopping became even more rapid. Between 2010 and 2019, e-commerce sales volume more than tripled as the reputability, affordability, and convenience of online buying grew.[5] As part of that shift, the way customers decide *what* to buy has changed as well.

In the past, customers would go to their favorite physical stores and purchase products they knew they liked, try new things they'd seen in advertisements, or be persuaded by in-store placements and merchandising to make an impulse purchase. But with online shopping, the store is essentially infinite, and you can't touch or examine the products.

The solution to this vastness is similar to what our friend Dany Levy attempted with *DailyCandy* back in 2000. A decade after the demise of Levy's brainchild, a new generation of content creators and product recommenders has risen to guide customers. Today's buyers, especially younger ones, are more inclined to trust third-party reviewers, influencers, and digital content publishers (bloggers, podcasters, review sites, and more) than they are to be swayed by a brand's glossy advertising.

This shift in behavior is backed by data—research shows that 34 percent of American consumers go online to read product or business reviews on a daily basis, and 79 percent of buyers trust online recommendations more than they trust recommendations from friends and family members.[6] As a result, publishers wield a significant amount of power in the new world of shopping.

An early pioneer in this space was Brian Kelly, known to many simply as "the Points Guy." In 2010, Kelly was working as a Wall Street HR professional, traveling constantly. Kelly not only accrued a lot of loyalty points as part of his professional travel but also began noticing some tricks to maximize the rewards a frequent traveler could earn. Before long, he had enough points to travel in first class for even his personal vacations.

Kelly's friends, seeing that he could offer real value with his expertise on the topic, urged him to start a blog on how to build up airline loyalty points. Eventually, credit card companies began paying Kelly to direct his audience to sign up for their airline rewards cards, turning Kelly's *The Points Guy* blog from a passion project into a lucrative full-time job. Kelly eventually sold *The Points Guy* to Bankrate for $20 million in 2012.[7]

Kelly was just one of a massive number of people who were using their passion and expertise to help people find the right products and services for them. Parenting blogs became more prevalent, offering practical child-rearing advice as well as carefully researched recommendations for strollers, cribs, and other essentials. Fitness blogs recommended both workout routines and workout equipment. Recipe bloggers could include references to certain cookware, ingredient services, or other products.

Once these publishers gained a loyal following, they could begin recommending products on a pay-for-outcomes basis, striking deals with companies to feature certain products in exchange for a fee or a commission for each sale. This transition was made possible in large part because technology made it much easier to track and attribute each individual transaction— publishers could now prove that their content was directly producing sales, and they could optimize and create new content accordingly.

Prominent publisher sites became so popular and lucrative that major media companies began adopting this pay-for-performance model for themselves. The New York Times Company purchased the popular product review and recommendation site Wirecutter for $30 million in 2016.[8] A year later, CNN launched their own product and services rating site, CNN Underscored. BuzzFeed, one of the savviest publishers of the digital media age, has been publishing product reviews in their listicles—monetized with affiliate links—for years and is on the verge of going public.

All these developments have created the retail world of today. More people shop online every year, and many increasingly seek out recommendations from product review sites they consider credible. These reviewers, in turn, are experienced in showcasing products authentically and persuasively and ask for payment only on a performance basis, not in the up-front fees *DailyCandy* required.

While you are likely aware of many of these changes, you may not have seized the crucial opportunity these shifts present: building commission-based partnerships with the top publishers in their industry.

Many publishers eschewed the affiliate model because they preferred guaranteed payment and there was plenty of demand for banner and CPM advertising. However, publishers of all kinds are quickly changing their tune as they see budgets shifting rapidly from brand marketing to performance, especially from the well-funded and high-growth DTC brands. This shift has caused a complete about-face, with many publishers now openly embracing the partnership marketing model as the key to unlocking value in their media assets and putting affiliate marketing at the center of their online business models.

Nowhere is this trend more evident than in the complete transformation of a once-failing publishing business into a data-driven, outcomes-oriented publisher—an organization that serves as a key advertising partner driving significant revenue for brands through a partnership marketing model.

From Stuck in the Past to Leading the Future

When Zillah Byng-Thorne became CEO of Future PLC in 2014, her friends and colleagues probably wondered what she was thinking, as she appeared to be taking the wheel of a sinking ship. The UK publishing giant, which specializes in content focused on how-to guides to help readers master new skills or manage technology and on research-driven, authoritative product recommendations, had seen its market capitalization shrink by over 90 percent to just over £30 million.

Fast-forward a few short years, and Future has dramatically changed its business model, earning nearly £500 million in revenue in 2020 and boasting a market capitalization of almost £4 billion. Byng-Thorne and her team achieved this exponential trajectory in part by embracing the outcome-based marketing techniques shared in this book. By partnering with advertisers on a commission basis, the company has reversed its course and driven massive sales volume for the brands that advertise in its publications.

Although Future's profitability had been shrinking, Byng-Thorne and her team recognized the value in their products: across their many publications, they had cultivated a massive audience of readers who trusted their expertise and were often looking for product recommendations. "I looked at the business and thought, what we have is this really helpful content that, fundamentally, people trust to help them make decisions that matter in their life," Byng-Thorne said.[9]

Future already had a large base of readers interested in learning new skills or discovering new products. What the business lacked before Byng-Thorne's tenure, however, was an ability to monetize its appeal to that audience—to use their authority to drive revenue through well-placed advertising.

In that regard, Byng-Thorne's previous experience proved invaluable. Before taking the helm at Future, she was an executive at Auto Trader. Auto Trader has long positioned itself as the last place potential car buyers go before finally heading to dealerships to hunt for a car to purchase, and it has built lucrative performance-based advertising relationships with auto dealers as a result. Byng-Thorne recognized that Future's expert recommendations could serve a similar purpose, effectively turning their digital publications into the last places potential customers visited before making a purchase. By linking directly to the products they recommended and receiving payment for conversions,

Future could create a steady stream of buyers for a brand and could monetize that flow of customers for their own benefit.

"People were coming to us for buying advice. Then, they were clicking out and needed to go and find that thing online. We figured, why don't we do the hard work for them, and bring the product into the page?" Byng-Thorne noted. "It will make a better user experience—it'll be more helpful—but it also allows us to participate in taking a commission for the transaction."

That revelation was the genesis of what became a game-changing revenue model for the business. Byng-Thorne and her team realized that placing tracking links in their digital content wasn't going to erode reader trust. If anything, it would improve the reader experience by making it easy to find and purchase the products they were recommending.

This simple shift in advertising strategy turned into a significant revenue stream for Future. In the past, they would include display advertisements prompting users to learn more about the products they were recommending—for example, placing banner ads for a certain laptop in a laptop recommendation article—but this new strategy meant they could place pertinent ads directly in the content. Not only did this make readers more likely to click on an advertised product, but it also established a clear link between Future's referrals and the eventual transaction. This link made it easier to attribute commissions and allowed Future to effectively position their marketing value to other brands as well.

Plus, once Future figured out the correct monetization structure, they could invest in creating much more content without the need to sell more advertising. Because each new piece of content presented the opportunity to drive more revenue, it was smart business to build their roster of expert writers and produce high-value content in areas where they knew there was demand. This development created great outcomes for Future and its partners, while also creating a better user experience for readers. Future, its readers, and its advertising partners all wanted to make it easier for people to buy the recommended products, and incentives were aligned for everyone involved.

You might think the majority of brands would be thrilled to be able to work with a prominent content publisher such as Future on an outcome basis. However, this wasn't always the case. Reflecting on the early years of Future's shift to outcome-based advertising, Byng-Thorne was surprised to see how resistant some businesses were to paying a commission rather than using the older method of banner ads and sponsored content. Some retailers viewed paying a commission as needlessly giving away a portion of revenue from each sale. However, Future was able to help brands understand outcome-based advertising as a reallocation of marketing dollars rather than a cannibalization of sales revenue. Customers had choices about where they bought their products, and Future played a key role in those decisions. Eventually, Future had the data to show potential advertisers what it was costing them to be excluded from the available options and how the price of being featured in one of Future's publications was greatly outpaced by the incremental revenue those placements generated for advertisers. The evidence was compelling, and Future has won over more brands with the model.

While Future's bet on this outcome-based advertising model was small at first, it's become a foundational piece of their business. Today, 20 percent of the company's revenue, including 40 percent of all web-based revenue, comes from commissions on linked products. Future has also produced £2 billion in annual sales for the brands that advertise through its various online publications.

As they've grown this vertical, Future has put considerable effort into determining which types of brands they want to partner with, taking care not to blur the lines between the editorial and monetization teams. Understanding how they determine which brands to partner with can help a business position itself to attract the best possible partners and get better outcomes as a result.

First, Future prioritizes working with brands that are trusted in their industries. When a retailer is linked in a Future publication, Future measures how many clicks they get as compared to similarly priced retailers to determine who their customers are most interested in buying from.

Next, Future evaluates how easy a brand makes it for users to purchase after they have clicked through to the site. Because the company gets paid only for sales that actually close, they want to ensure that customers can easily purchase a product after they've left Future's page. For example, Amazon's one-click purchase option is the gold standard for low-friction e-commerce buying, and more companies should emulate that approach if they want access to the best content partners. If a brand has a very poor conversion rate, it's likely to be placed lower on the list of buying options.

On the brand side, Byng-Thorne noted that companies should be careful about placing ads with the correct media partners and publishers. Reputable, effective marketing partners don't want to advertise just any product on their sites—they want to feature ads relevant to the content they produce. For example, a computer recommendation website wouldn't try to persuade its readers to buy scuba-diving equipment, because doing so would dilute their audience trust and likely not even garner enough sales to make the placement worth it for either the blogger or the brand placing the ad.

However, when brands match the right publisher with the right product, the opportunities are significant. In fact, Byng-Thorne expects that, as lucrative as the channel has been thus far, it will only continue to scale as more brands recognize the revenue potential. "The trend continues at scale. This year has been a quickening, for retail in particular," said Byng-Thorne. "Media publishers can become the virtual High Street." What Byng-Thorne is suggesting is that brands that partner with publishers are positioning themselves as prominent options for the massive number of customers who primarily shop online, helping to capture customers' attention in a world increasingly dependent upon e-commerce.

"People are going to want to build a brand, and I think that part of advertising will always continue," Byng-Thorne said. "But outside of that, [performance-based] marketing budgets will increase. Why would you not spend your money on an ROI where you only pay if you get the outcome you're looking for?"

Byng-Thorne's most essential observation is that when brands realize how strong the ROI is for outcome-based advertising, they tend to want more of it. In fact, Future has even seen long-standing brand partners willing to pay a higher commission per sale because they know they will make up for that spending with more revenue.

While Future has been proactive in shifting its model, many

publishers that have previously relied on banner display ads are beginning to feel the pinch as market forces take hold. Supply and demand are always closely linked; as more advertisers shift their budgets to acquisition-oriented marketing, the demand for partners that want access to those budgets will continue to increase.

Future's story also illustrates two additional key points for brands to understand. First, publishers have a level of credibility with potential customers that brands want to leverage. Even customers who are wary of being sold to are often more willing to buy a product recommended by a publication they trust. Second, it's easy to expand this model after it has been proven to work. A company can increase its investment in this type of outcome-based initiative without facing the risk of their budget outpacing their returns.

Publishers are increasingly adopting this type of marketing model and have found many brands that have been convinced of the model's effectiveness. Today, there exists a vast network of potential marketing partners, from individually owned mom blogs to giants like BuzzFeed and CNN Underscored, who can be engaged in pay-for-performance partnerships that can be tracked via software technology.

Don't React; Act

While some brands have gotten ahead of the partnership mar-keting curve, many have neglected to adjust their marketing strategies to fit the times. We are so far removed from the early days of Barbie, but so many brands are still trying to apply the same playbook by chasing too many popular channels and fail-ing to connect their spending to the desired outcomes.

Today, the most entrenched marketing platforms still aren't optimized around results. A savvy business with a data-driven, performance-oriented marketing strategy can still find itself get-ting caught up in an unwinnable auction dominated by some of the world's largest, most powerful companies. The game of dig-ital marketing has been tilted heavily in advertisers' favor, and your business needs to recognize when it's been swept up in the auction mania.

Key Takeaways

- ▶ The rise of DTC brands has made direct customer acquisi-tion more valuable than ever. This is especially true for sub-scription brands that get high lifetime value from a single customer.
- ▶ The explosion of DTC brands was matched with a simi-lar growth in publishers offering curated product reviews,

allowing brands to target customers in a more authentic, effective way.

► The best publishers have figured out how to enhance their content and marketing placements to optimize the user experience and drive better results for brands.

Up Next

Why marketing in traditional digital channels today is akin to bidding in the world's biggest auction—and how your business can avoid the trap.

3.

Step Right Up: The World's Biggest Auction

"The smartest side to take in a bidding war is the losing side."

—WARREN BUFFETT

In the early 1970s, an economics graduate student at the University of Rochester named Richard Thaler made a surprising observation about one of his professors, Richard Rosett. Rosett was an avid wine collector and a frequent buyer at auctions. As the story goes, Rosett would never sell a bottle from his collection for less than $100 and would never pay more than $35 for a bottle of similar quality. Essentially, Rosett was expecting others to pay three times more than he would for an equivalent bottle, counting on an auction to drive up the price. Rosett, an economist so respected that he went on to become the dean of the University of Chicago's Booth School of Business, was banking on people behaving irrationally in an auction environment.[1]

When you dissect the auction format, Rosett's bet makes sense. Auctions are designed to turn selling an item into an instantaneously competitive process, pushing buyers to drive up the price in real time rather than carefully assessing what an item is worth and paying for it accordingly. A seller can get a much better price this way than they would by negotiating with an individual buyer.

Auctions are also particularly effective at selling goods of uncertain value. If we are competing for a luxury item, such as a painting or an antique, it's difficult to place an objective price on such a uniquely valuable good. Instead, the value is set by the perception of others, and auction buyers must accommodate a fast-rising price to stay in the running.

Furthermore, auctions capitalize on two psychological tendencies: a habit of fixating on things we can potentially own and a hatred of losing things we possess. In effect, auctions create these two feelings several times over. A person places a bid and begins to picture themselves owning the item. Then, as soon as another bidder tops their price, they feel the sting of losing that same item and bid higher. This cycle tempts people to pay more than they normally would, because losing feels intolerable in the moment.

The data demonstrates that people tend to overpay in an auction environment. In a study of eBay auctions conducted in 2007, economists Young Han Lee and Ulrike Malmendier discovered that, when including shipping costs, the average eBay auction winner overpaid by 73 percent in their winning bid for a given item.[2] They could have paid considerably less by buying the exact same item through a fixed-price listing.

Fortunately, most of us don't regularly find ourselves in auctions where our competitive instincts could lose us millions. But imagine if your business was caught in that exact same auction environment, with your budget and revenue at stake. Would you trust yourself to get good ROI when bidding against your competitors? Would you expect the auctioneer to share your incentives?

If this scenario sounds like a nightmare, here's the wake-up call: your business is probably in this environment already. Many of the popular digital marketing channels today have become giant auctions, and your business needs to know how to get out before the price becomes too high.

Going Once, Going Twice...Gone

As you may recall from the introduction, *DailyCandy* demonstrated a repetitive dysfunctional cycle that occurs in each new marketing channel. Every time a new channel shows promising ROI, it becomes flooded with buyers, driving the price beyond the point of profitability and leaving many brands paying for marketing that's not worth the money.

The rise of digital marketing has intensified this cycle; the window of profitability for the most popular channel of the day is perilously small and shrinking. Even emerging, high-value channels get flooded with buyers quickly, and increasingly, more marketing inventory is purchased in an auction environment. For example, Facebook and Google do not sell their advertisements at a fixed rate. Instead, they have advertisers bid against one another, ultimately awarding placements to the brands that are willing to pay more.

The impact that this auction environment has on the marketing ecosystem cannot be overstated. To stay ahead of the competition, you need to be fast, nimble, and well capitalized. You also better have sophisticated bidding tools.

We rationally know that auctions can inflate prices above the value we get in return, but when you hear, for example, that a brand has earned a surge of web traffic from a certain channel, it can make you feel foolish for not getting in the game. However, while you can see where your competitors are investing their marketing dollars, what you don't know is whether they are getting their money's worth in return. You can watch the game, but the scoreboard that matters most is hidden. In fact, many brands are bidding competitively for marketing placements without even knowing the revenue those campaigns will create. This practice creates a problem that economists refer to as "the winner's curse." As University of Chicago economist Eric Budish put it:

> If you know with 100 percent confidence what your value for an item is, and you bid the most for something because you have a really high value for it, that's fine. You might be paying a lot, but at least the pricing is going to be right. But if there's some uncertainty [as] to what the value of an object is—or what the value of a keyword is, or what the value of an advertising slot is— the winner is going to be whoever is most aggressive in valuation. Unless they're correcting for their behavioral tendencies, they will overbid.[3]

In short, winning an auction is great if you know the value of what you're bidding for and bid accordingly. But if you bid simply to win, without a clear value of what you're getting, you run a high risk of paying more than the item is worth.

One way to avoid the winner's curse is to ignore the auction altogether. This is why you see many savvy companies increasingly avoiding auction-based digital channels and resorting to tried-and-true tactics with less competition, such as catalogs and email. These companies know prices drop when there isn't as much demand, and ROI rises as a result.

It's always been better to avoid the trap of overinvesting in channels that offer *input* metrics, such as impressions and clicks, and instead invest money in programs tied to demonstrable *outcomes*, such as sales, leads, or other important conversions. Yet so many businesses struggle to maintain a competitive advantage because they are constantly falling in love with the method and not the corresponding outcome.

Most marketers today know what outcomes they are trying to achieve; they likely have clear metrics for how many leads they want to generate, how many new customers they want to acquire, or even how much revenue they want to drive through their marketing initiatives. The problem is that they get caught up in the auction, bidding more and more without even realizing that winning often isn't worth the price.

Bidding on the Triopoly

Not surprisingly, the biggest auctions in digital marketing today occur through the Triopoly of Amazon, Facebook, and Google. According to a study by eMarketer, 70 percent of all digital marketing spend flows through these three giants.[4] They have created marketplaces of instantaneous bidding that drive faster price escalation, greater profit for the platforms, and, as a result, less sustainable ROI for your business. For example, according to their own earnings report, Facebook's average ad price increased by 47 percent between 2020 and 2021; that's likely far more than the corresponding increase in profit for the businesses that are advertising on the platform.[5]

Marketing through the Triopoly also often means working with several intermediaries, paying hidden fees, and not interacting with the platforms directly. Not only are companies paying more for their digital advertising each year, but they are paying a significant portion of their budget to middlemen.

Another problem brands face when marketing through the Triopoly is that larger brands often have an advantage over smaller competitors. Companies that have huge budgets, high-priced consultants, and the best possible technological tools can calibrate their bidding to avoid the bidding wars for popular "head" terms and instead pursue sophisticated mid- and long-tail strategies, avoiding the most competitive terms and placements. For example, rather than bidding $1 per click for the keyword "online shoes," a sophisticated advertiser might bid $0.10 per click on a collection of hundreds or thousands of longer-tail terms such as "women's basketball shoes," "men's leisure shoes," or even "size 8 red men's Converse shoes."

Just as tax law changes often affect the wealthiest the least because they have the experts and resources to shift strategies and avoid the impact, many of the companies with the deepest pockets are best positioned to thrive in the auction frenzy. Small and medium-sized companies must recognize that they may not have the resources to compete effectively in the Triopoly game.

Because bidding escalates faster than ever in the new world of digital marketing, each phase of the game goes faster and reaches the end sooner. The cost of bidding on the Triopoly is only going up, and just as a run on housing eventually leaves prospective homeowners priced out, many buyers are about to find themselves priced out of the digital marketplace entirely or forced to significantly reduce their expectations of returns.

Name Your Price

Fortunately, the outcome-based model of partnership marketing allows brands to avoid this type of auction environment. Rather than bidding into an opaque auction for placements, brands, or the agencies that represent them, brands set a default rate that ensures an acceptable level of profitability, then recruit partners who are willing to deliver at that price.

As we mentioned earlier in this chapter, it's difficult to set a fair price for an item of unclear value. In a partnership marketing program, the value of the initiative is clear, because the outcomes the partner must achieve are set in advance. When brands have to pay only after they get the outcomes they want, it's easier to ensure a fair price. And because partnership marketing programs cost only a portion of the revenue they generate, budgets can be essentially unlimited.

That pricing model ensures that brands are always aware of how the commissions they are investing connect to their overall ROI. Publishers cannot escalate the price drastically without brands noticing that their profits are decreasing. While a hot, well-funded brand in a competitive marketplace may become convinced that a pricey Facebook ad could be worth the money, especially if they see their competition doing the same, a rational, acquisition-oriented marketer would not pay $1,500 in commissions for $1,000 in one-time revenue.

Another benefit of partnership marketing is that, because the model is heavily relationship driven, partners aren't solely interested in chasing the highest price when evaluating potential partnerships with brands. Many partners depend on brands for their livelihood and, as a result, will gravitate to brands and programs that pay on time, are responsive to requests, treat them fairly when a mistake is made, and proactively share new opportunities. Additionally, many partners are just as interested in the quality of a brand's product or service and whether it resonates with them and their audience. This is true both of big, editorial-based publishers and smaller influencers or bloggers who have their own personal brands and interests.

Big marketing channels like Amazon, Facebook, and Google won't deviate from the auction model as long as it continues to be so profitable for them. Partnership marketing offers brands an opportunity to invest their budgets in a different economic model that is more focused on outcomes.

It's difficult to find value if you're spending too much time at the auction house. This is especially true for venture-backed start-ups, which step into these auction environments with plenty of investor money to burn and a need to show topline revenue growth. Carving out an effective position while competing in today's environment requires deciding carefully where to spend your limited resources.

Key Takeaways

▸ The most popular marketing channels—especially the Triopoly of Facebook, Google, and Amazon—leverage auction-based pricing that makes it easy to get caught up in a bidding war.

▸ The annual price increases for these platforms far exceed the profitability growth rates of most advertisers.

▶ The Triopoly's pricing model benefits bigger brands with higher budgets, specialized consultants, and other financial advantages.

▶ Partnership marketing is relationship driven and outcome based, avoiding the real-time auction.

Up Next

How partnership marketing can help brands compete with the Goliath of retail.

4.

Facing the Colossus

"What's dangerous is not to evolve."

—JEFF BEZOS

In one way or another today, every brand is competing with the same black-and-orange giant: Amazon. This is especially true in the retail world, which Amazon has completely upended in the past twenty-five years. And while Amazon is known for its low prices and remarkable shipping power, they provide perhaps the stiffest competition in marketing.

Amazon spent over $22 billion on marketing in 2020,[1] and 197 million people purchase from their platform each month.[2] With their resources and a direct relationship with a monthly customer base the size of Russia, Amazon is a formidable competitor for almost any business. Remember that if you invest in digital marketing channels like display ads, paid search, and other input-driven models, you may very well be competing with a Goliath that can outspend you exponentially for the same target customer.

To paraphrase the popular saying: If brands can't beat Amazon in traditional marketing, should they consider joining them? Amazon has created a network of millions of third-party sellers who can attract and sell to customers through the world's most popular retail platform. Rather than competing with Amazon, many brands have just opted to use Amazon's massive marketing operation to drive sales for them and pay Amazon to take on that role in what is a variation of partnership marketing.

However, Amazon isn't the only competition third-party sellers need to worry about. The fastest growing part of Amazon's business is Amazon Marketplace; today, 55 percent of all items sold through Amazon are sold by third parties, not by Amazon directly.[3] Brands that sell through Amazon must compete with other third-party sellers in the world's biggest retail colosseum. In 2015, the *Guardian* shared a story of a family-owned bike shop called Swinnerton Cycles that sold on Amazon at a loss, effectively as a form of advertising.[4] They simply could not be profitable on the platform due to the selling costs and the pressure to race other brands to the bottom in price setting.

Amazon has tremendous customer loyalty, and the size of its marketing apparatus creates a bit of a dilemma. Most businesses, even successful ones, cannot outspend Amazon in traditional marketing channels or erode their market share through conventional means. If they sell through Amazon, they enter fierce competition with other brands, including possibly Amazon itself.

Plus, in cases where a brand *can* sell effectively through Amazon, the customer often becomes Amazon's customer and not their own. Part of the reason for this is that Amazon shares limited customer data with third-party sellers.

At the end of the day, every business, especially in retail, must understand the challenges they face when they compete with Amazon and many of the other emerging marketplaces head-to-head and carefully determine their marketing strategy accordingly. This is where partnership marketing comes in.

In partnership marketing, Amazon's strength—its sheer scale—also presents an opportunity for smaller brands. Amazon has what is almost certainly the largest affiliate marketing program in the world, the Amazon Associates program, with what has been estimated to be more than one million affiliate partners.

First, because of the size of the program, Amazon must understandably rely on widespread automation. Therefore, the vast majority of the publishers in the program will not have a direct relationship with someone at Amazon. Smaller brands can step into the void in areas where that personalization and a human connection can make a difference, especially given that, as noted in chapter 2, many partners are looking for more than just dollars in the programs they join. These brands are able to work more closely with partners than Amazon can, offering specific ways to optimize performance, more relevant content to entice readers, and potential access to offers and exclusive opportunities that would not otherwise be possible.

Second, when Amazon makes a shift in its affiliate program strategy, it tends to have a big impact. For example, Amazon made major changes to its program early in the COVID-19 pandemic, changing its commission structure and removing large publishers when it was faced with more demand than it could fulfill. Remember, with the bulk of Amazon's sales of non-Amazon-branded products coming from third-party sellers, Amazon is effectively paying affiliates out of the 5 to 15 percent commission it gets on each of these marketplace sales rather than out of the 85 to 95 percent of profits the brands keep for themselves. While these decisions make sense for a program of Amazon's size, they can be disruptive for partners, especially those who have not diversified their partnerships. Many brands used this as an opportunity to reach out to new publishers who had never worked directly with the brand before and saw a big uptick in the growth of their partnership programs as a result—growth that largely continued even after Amazon reversed some of its commission changes, due to the new relationships that were formed.

Finally, partnership marketing may also be changing how Amazon thinks about their partnership program for these third-party sellers on their platform. As of the writing of this book, Amazon is testing an initiative to open up its attribution pixel, allowing transactions sent by publishers in outside partnership marketing programs to be tracked and reported through to conversion for the first time. This means that brands that *are* selling on Amazon can possibly create their own partnership programs on the Amazon platform, where they own and manage the relationships with publishers directly. In these programs, brands pay the commissions and influence how these publishers market their products.

This trend makes a ton of sense for Amazon and other marketplaces such as Apple and Walmart, which should be very willing to stand aside and let brands absorb the direct costs of partnership marketing for their own products, because they generate the majority of the revenue in a transaction. This change would allow smaller and midsize brands to have the leverage of Amazon or other marketplace platforms and work more personally with publishers who promote their products specifically. We are in the process of helping several brands set up and test these programs, and we expect them to become mainstream fairly soon.

Key Takeaways

▶ To an extent, every brand is competing with Amazon, and attempting to beat them head-to-head in traditional marketing channels may not be the best strategy.

▶ Partnership marketing offers the ability for brands to sidestep direct competition with Amazon by leaning on partners that share their incentives.

Up Next

What new data privacy laws mean for business and how partnership marketing can help adjust to them.

5.

The Privacy Problem

"Human beings are not meant to lose
their anonymity and privacy."

—SARAH CHALKE

Over a decade ago, a furious customer stormed into a Target in
Minnesota and asked to see a manager. He demanded to know
why his teenage daughter had received a mailer of coupons that
offered discounts on maternity clothing, baby clothes, and cribs.
The customer was outraged that Target appeared to be pushing
his daughter, who was still in high school, to get pregnant. The
manager was stunned as well, apologized profusely, and considered the situation defused. But a few days later, when the manager called to offer a second apology, what he heard in response

was even more surprising. "It turns out there's been some activities in my house I haven't been completely aware of," the customer said. "She's due in August. I owe you an apology."[1]

Unbeknownst to both the customer and the manager, Target had taken the business adage "know your customer" to an extreme. They knew this particular customer better than the customer's own dad did.

In the year before that incident, a Target data wiz named Andrew Pole had built a marketing algorithm to identify pregnant customers based upon their recent purchases and send them coupons for products women often need when they are expecting: baby clothes, nursery furniture, even supplements like zinc and folic acid. The pregnancy-themed mailer wasn't just blind luck; it was an intentional, data-driven marketing campaign.

If you're unsettled by the idea of a retail giant knowing a person is pregnant before their own family does, you're not alone. In fact, Target recognized at the time that some customers would be creeped out by this data use, so they decided to place the precisely targeted ads next to dissimilar products to make them appear random.

Today, this type of personal-data-driven tactic is more common but no less disconcerting for many customers. Everyone knows the experience of looking at a product on a brand's website or even talking about it with a friend and then seeing ads for that product everywhere they go online. In 2017, the BBC published an article of first-person accounts of uncannily well-targeted ads, including from an engaged couple who was bombarded by wedding ads before even announcing their recent engagement to friends and family.[2]

As a result of stories like this, a global reckoning on data privacy is threatening to dictate the future of business and especially of marketing. The first shot across the bow of the data-privacy fight was the implementation of the European Union's General Data Protection Regulation (GDPR), a comprehensive set of consumer information laws. In addition to creating a litany of data-security regulations for companies to follow, GDPR also cracked down on how companies collect and use personally identifiable information (PII).

In the past, web users were either unaware of just how much personal data was being harvested by the websites they visited or simply accepted this data collection as a cost of the free internet. However, that attitude is changing. Customers are now wary of companies' PII use; a 2020 study by the California privacy compliance technology firm TRUSTe found that 92 percent of American customers cite data security and privacy as a concern. Another study by the Chartered Institute of Marketing found 57 percent of American customers don't trust companies to use their data responsibly.[3] Companies all around the world should consider the possibility that many of their PII-driven marketing initiatives may become much more difficult, if not impossible, in a more private world.

Have you considered how data regulations or customer attitudes toward privacy may affect your business? As this chapter illustrates, the marketing implications of a potential crackdown on data collection are enormous, and partnership marketing is uniquely positioned to perform well in this new environment because it is less dependent on personally identifiable customer data.

Regulation Nation

GDPR was a game changer in Europe, and non-European brands should pay attention to it as well. By understanding the basics of the law, leaders can extrapolate what future data regulations may look like, how they might affect their businesses, and how they need to proactively adapt to these changes.

The actual documentation of GDPR is eighty-eight pages long, so this is hardly a full summary of what the law requires. However, the most important impacts on marketing are as follows:

- ▸ Companies must request clear consent to collect personal data from customers or site visitors.
- ▸ Companies must allow users to opt out of having their data sold to other companies.
- ▸ Companies must allow users to be "forgotten" or to request that they be deleted from a company's database.[4]

Very similar provisions are also required by the California Consumer Privacy Act (CCPA).[5] While we can't be sure, it is reasonable to assume that any additional state or federal regulations will include these core protections as well.

Regulations like GDPR pose the biggest threat to businesses that rely upon data-driven advertising. These are the types of companies that sell ads that automatically follow specific customers from site to site, relying upon a constantly growing trove of consumer data. Web users are often more wary of giving their personal data to third-party firms rather than directly to companies they like.

As a result of this wave of regulations, brands are currently in a race to collect their own data, using GDPR-compliant first-party cookies to collect information with consumer approval. Simultaneously, brands must also use their customer data carefully to build trust with their audiences and ensure that customers don't wish to be forgotten. Using first-party data for invasive targeted marketing will likely create the same customer distrust that led to more regulation in the first place. Brands should try to use their data in less suspicious ways by showing ads in places where they are expected, or even useful, for customers.

The future of data-driven advertising is built on proper context. It feels much less invasive for a prospective customer to see a BMW ad when they are searching for luxury cars rather than getting a BMW ad because of their demographic profile and friends' purchases, even after they recently bought a Mercedes and aren't shopping for a car.

Current and future regulations regarding PII will challenge all online marketing that is based on tracking. However, partnership marketing has some unique attributes that make it far less vulnerable.

The Cookie Crumbles

For years, websites and browsers have harvested information from customers via tracking codes known as cookies. A cookie collects information about users and the websites they visit, perhaps without their knowledge or permission. This data is then combined with first-party data to build an entire profile of the prospective customer and their behavior.

There's an important distinction between first-party cookies and third-party cookies. A first-party cookie is one placed by the website owner, allowing it to retain PII learned about that customer's behavior on the website. Brands often get customer data by asking site visitors to accept cookies or by inviting them to create an account on the site and provide their e-mail address and other contact information. A third-party cookie collects and retains that same type of visitor data, but it is collected by someone other than the brand itself, such as an advertiser or data firm. These third-party cookies almost never give users the chance to opt in or out.

Due to changing privacy laws and consumer demand, the third-party cookie is on its way to extinction. Google Chrome, the world's most-used browser, will soon block third-party cookies.[6] Companies that lack a system for collecting, storing, and analyzing customer data are particularly vulnerable to this change. And third-party advertisers and marketers will see their own data collection systems crunched and will face severe limitations on some of their top marketing tactics.

Perhaps the most jeopardized tactic is retargeting. This popular advertising tactic has an ad seller use a massive cache of third-party data to automatically determine which ads to show which customers. This tactic is growing in popularity; researchers at the Delhi School of Marketing found that 68 percent of marketing agencies and 49 percent of brands allocate budget to the tactic.[7] However, use of this tactic dropped by 50 percent in Europe within a year of GDPR's passage.[8]

You've surely experienced retargeting before, even if you haven't used it yourself. Think of a situation where you've gone to a brand's website and considered buying a product—say, an electric toothbrush—but ultimately decided not to buy it. However, you've left a data trail that's tied you to that toothbrush permanently. Automated ad sellers begin placing ads everywhere you go online, from your Facebook newsfeed to banners on every site you visit. Your data has become a bulwark for an advertising firm's strategy.

Now that we're decades into the internet age, many web users expect companies to retain a certain amount of their personal data. But when a company uses location and demographic data to estimate a person's preferences—for example, showing someone an ad for a product the friend they've just met for lunch has bought because they can discern through geotargeting that they are together—it creates an Orwellian feeling of creepiness reminiscent of the Target example above.

The Rich Get Richer

There's a natural question that comes from these explorations of privacy (or the lack thereof): Are all companies and marketing platforms facing the same degree of threat?

Perhaps unsurprisingly, the answer is no. In fact, the privacy concerns may end up stacking the deck even more in favor of the Triopoly and the other largest players.

As mentioned above, tighter PII regulations like GDPR and CCPA are especially restrictive of the collection of third-party data. Companies can still collect information on their own customers, and the vast majority of people who spend time on Amazon, Facebook, and Google are existing customers of those firms. They simply need to be transparent about this data collection and give users the right to have their data deleted if they desire. Most people are willing to give up a bit of their personal information in exchange for goods and services they want, and many are willing to accept first-party cookies to have a more personalized experience on a brand's site.

The bottom line is that first-party data is going to become far more valuable as privacy regulations are developed, and Amazon, Facebook, and Google are some of the world's best at collecting this type of data. A massive number of customers will continue to provide their information to access Amazon's world-class shipping or to use Google and Facebook for free.

Because Amazon, Facebook, and Google are far less reliant on third-party data, their share of the traditional marketing pie will only grow larger, and their ability to set high prices will only increase. Plus, if these three giants ever find themselves in violation of data protection laws, they have significant legal teams to contest the charges and the resources to absorb hefty fines that would significantly impair a smaller company.

These privacy-driven changes are making it more difficult for some brands to compete in traditional marketing channels. Fortunately, partnership marketing offers a solution.

Context and Commerce

Before the age of automated ad selling and retargeted advertisements, digital marketing did not provoke this degree of concern about privacy. This was partly because many digital ads were tied to paid search campaigns—a customer would search for a specific product or service and see ads for those things.

Even early display ads were more contextual rather than personalized. Companies tended to advertise where there was a highly interested group of buyers—such as placing a perfume ad on a women's lifestyle site or a Budweiser ad on ESPN.com. The advertisements didn't trigger as many privacy concerns for users because the products were often well suited to the sites and publications where those ads were placed. The ad placements intuitively made sense to users, in part because they were based on contextual decisions by marketers and merchandisers, not devised from troves of customer data.

In this new environment of privacy prioritization, brands can get results by shifting back to ads that have this type of contextual comfort. In fact, one of the core value propositions for the partnership marketing model is that it connects brands with niche publishers, influencers with trusting audiences, and other partners that can credibly speak to a curated audience without making prospective customers think they are being spied on.

For example, with partnership marketing, a retail brand that sells athletic shoes might partner with the publisher of a top sneaker review website. Unlike an automated ad seller or marketing agency, this publisher can advertise products without relying on a massive cache of customer data. The blog's readers trust the publisher's recommendations, expect referrals, and visit the blog specifically to learn which shoes they should buy. The publisher and brand are teaming up to turn content into commerce through context.

When a shoe brand advertises its product on the publisher's blog, readers are far less likely to question why those ads are being shown, as they might with traditional display ads based on their personal browsing history or profile. Customer data is not necessary for the sneaker blogger, because they have the appropriate context. They don't need information about what websites their readers visit, what they've purchased previously, or where they live. The blogger or influencer assumes that their readers are interested in buying the shoes they are reviewing, and they can naturally include a purchase link. In doing so, they drive highly relevant and interested customers to the brand.

Similarly, companies don't need to know who the sneaker blog's readers are or even how big their readership is to be willing to partner. If the publisher creates content in a context that is aligned with the brand's product and is willing to work on a pay-for-performance model, there is very little risk to a partnership.

Partnership marketing is built on serving advertisements in an ideal context by leveraging publishers with well-cultivated audiences who are showing interest in learning more about specific products. The model doesn't rely on a deep well of PII to be effective.

Just as you wouldn't allow your business to become over-leveraged in debt, it would be unwise to allow your company to become overdependent on data you may not be able to rely on in the future. Just as it is recommended to have a diversified financial portfolio, it is important to diversify your marketing budget by investing in channels less dependent on customer data. The more you can prepare for a stricter era of data protection regulations now, the more you'll outperform your unprepared competitors in the future.

Key Takeaways

- Consumers value data protection and privacy more and more, and this has significant implications for data-driven marketing.
- Regulations such as GDPR and the CCPA have already made significant changes to how companies can collect and use data, and they may be harbingers of what's to come.
- Partnership marketing allows companies to target narrow demographics and well-primed audiences without relying on secretly collected data.

Up Next

How partnership marketing works on a detailed level.

6.

The New Partnership Marketing

"Marketing's job is never done. It's about perpetual motion. We must continue to innovate every day."

—BETH COMSTOCK

Throughout history, we have seen new technological advancements initially deployed by looking into the past, only to really create new opportunities once the technology was applied in different ways. For example, the first movies were often more akin to filmed theatrical productions, before filmmakers learned how to use cameras in new ways and changed the trajectory of the movie industry.

We see this same process of innovation often in business.

The invention of financial lending began as a simple way to help people buy valuable things without tons of cash, but it created an industry that powers the global economy. The computer was created to help with business as it was done fifty years ago, and now it is the foundation of the totally different way we work today. Technology dictates how we live, work, and shop.

Technological innovation has built the new definition of partnership marketing, improving upon the narrow channel of affiliate marketing and the manual world of partnerships that has existed in business for as long as we can remember. If you want to understand how partnership marketing works and what it can do for your business, it's essential to understand the changes in technology and pricing that have built the channel's promising future. In this chapter, you'll get a clear understanding of how partnership marketing technology has evolved, how those technological changes have optimized the partnership marketing business model, and what that optimization means for your business today and tomorrow.

Affiliate Marketing Revisited

In chapter 1, we provided a brief overview of partnership marketing and its precursor, affiliate marketing. Let's revisit the evolution of this model with a bit more detail with examples to explain how partnership marketing reached this point and discuss the future implications for companies of all sizes.

At its most basic level, affiliate marketing is a way to pay partners who drive certain results for your business. An affiliate can be any person or group that has an audience and potential influence over the desired outcome, whether that is a purchase, a lead, or anything else. They can be publishers of specialty blogs, product comparison or review sites, media conglomerates, mobile apps, and more. However, even other companies that sell products can be potential affiliates, through methods such as post-purchase recommendation emails or confirmation pages.

When done well, affiliate marketing is a low-risk way to build a business, allowing companies to pay only after they've gotten the outcomes they want. Typically, brands pay a percentage of a sale or a fixed price for a lead that their affiliate generates. The technology behind affiliate marketing is also beginning to be used in new and different ways.

Affiliate marketing has always been technology enabled, with a business model historically reliant upon affiliate networks and governed by a performance-based fee model. As discussed earlier, an affiliate network is a technology platform that "hosts" affiliate programs—including creative copy, product feeds, and links—recruits well-vetted affiliates, and matches them to brands based on product, budget, and program goals. These networks consolidate all the brand's affiliate relationships in one place and handle the other various administrative functions of program management, such as compliance and tax payments. The network consistently tracks and reports on all these affiliate partnerships and ensures that affiliates are paid for the outcomes they deliver to brands. They are the trusted intermediaries for both affiliates and brands, similar to an escrow agent.

Affiliate networks provide a vital function—they allow a brand to utilize a platform with many affiliates without having to manage every individual partner directly, saving companies the hassle of maintaining hundreds of one-on-one, manual relationships. Affiliates can also join many different programs on a single platform and benefit from integrated reporting and payments.

When a brand works with an affiliate network, the two parties launch what is essentially a cobranded, joint venture. While this model has many benefits, there are also some corresponding drawbacks.

First, brands that work with an affiliate network must understandably surrender a certain degree of control to reap the rewards of the network effect.

Second, because networks represent both the brands and the publishers who operate on their platform, there is a potential for conflicts of interest, as discussed briefly in chapter 1.

The prevailing pricing model of many affiliate networks,

which has existed for more than twenty years, also isn't the right solution for every brand. Networks have historically taken payment as a percentage of either all the revenue driven on the platform or all the commissions paid to publishers. At the peak of the network model, that fee was as high as 3 percent of sales or 30 percent of all commissions. For example, if a company were to offer a 10 percent affiliate commission for sales generated through the network, a $100 sale would earn a payout of $10 for the affiliate/publisher, with an additional $3 going to the network. Generally, this type of network fee is a fixed rate applied to all publishers on the platform, whether the publisher was recruited by the network or added to the program by the brand directly. In either case, the network still gets paid for the revenue or leads each affiliate generates and receives the same percentage in perpetuity. Of course, the opposite can be true as well—if a brand decides to cut commissions substantially, the network takes a corresponding hit to their share of revenue. The prevailing pricing model can lead to suboptimal outcomes for either side, depending on the circumstances.

Working with an affiliate network is similar to using a shared office space; there are trade-offs to the model itself. For example, working in a coworking space provides great connectivity and allows a small company to be part of something bigger, have more networking opportunities, and have access to shared resources it could not otherwise afford. At the same time, you probably wouldn't want to share a workplace, printer, and break room with your biggest competitor.

Consider an example: let's say a brand called the Acme Company decides to launch an affiliate program. They partner with a network, Affiliates 'R Us, to manage their entire program. The program works well, and the Acme Company is happy with the sales generated. The Acme Company receives substantial benefits from their arrangement with Affiliates 'R Us. They have access to the large pool of publishers already on the platform who are looking to join new programs, which is particularly helpful for emerging brands. The network's real-time payment and tracking system also saves the brand significant overhead costs and effort.

Acme Company experiences some trade-offs in this model as well. First, the partners in an affiliate network are visible to all other brands in the network and can be recruited by the managers of other programs who might be competitors, depending on the network's operating and privacy policies. As a result, a company may inadvertently be helping their competitors, especially if new partners they've brought directly into their network program end up getting referred to competitors directly or indirectly. Referring back to our shared-office analogy, if your company worked in a coworking space and another business in that same space kept poaching your employees or calling candidates whose résumés you left on the copy machine, you'd have some valid concerns about the arrangement.

Another factor to consider—something the industry has not wanted to address for a long time—is that the performance-fee pricing model eventually becomes more of a tax than a true performance incentive under certain conditions, especially if a small and consistent group of publishers drives the majority of sales year over year. The fee is even more of a tax when a brand's program matures and the company starts identifying and recruiting more of their own partners directly. For example, if the Acme Company recruits an influential blogger into their network-based affiliate program to leverage the network's tech platform, they pay that same perpetual performance fee for every commission the blogger earns. Acme wants and values the tracking and payment aspects of the network's platform, but they aren't really excited about paying Affiliates 'R Us a high-performance fee for a partner they recruited, onboarded, and manage themselves. The level of fee does not correlate with the services being rendered, especially for many enterprise brands with established programs.

To crystalize this concept further, imagine if Salesforce charged a 10 percent performance fee for its customer relationship management (CRM) software, based on the number of new clients you acquired using its system. Clients would agree to that structure only if Salesforce constantly provided new leads into the CRM system; clients would be resistant to paying a 10 percent performance fee just for the software's functionality and would rather pay a flat licensing fee. Clients would be especially reticent to pay such a performance fee if Salesforce also shared the client's prospects or leads with other Salesforce clients.

We don't know a single sales leader whose compensation plan includes perpetual commissions on clients they brought in years ago; almost all salespeople need to keep selling new clients and don't get credit for old ones past a certain point. But this is effectively how brands have paid networks for publisher performance for over two decades. Brands are starting to realize that, at some point, these incumbent partners should move into a fixed or lower price tier if new or incremental value isn't being created beyond the core tracking and payment functionality.

There are also limitations to the model for more business-development-oriented or direct relationships. An Acme program run by Affiliates 'R Us, with cobranding, may not give Acme the desired level of flexibility and control in these types of partnerships. This lack of control can cause issues when brands and partners end up in disputes over program violations, deceptive tactics, or outright fraud. The network technically represents both parties and understandably wants to protect relationships with publishers who work across many programs. That dynamic doesn't sit very well with some larger brands who are used to very tightly controlled licensing and partnership deals that have strict compliance terms, which are enforced unilaterally.

Acme can address this potential conflict of interest by building and managing their own direct partnerships outside their affiliate program, allowing them to circumvent the performance fee and the need to cobrand. Of course, these partnerships need to be managed, tracked, and paid manually; while this can work for a small number of partnerships, it is not very scalable. In these cases, what brands want is the same affiliate network technology but a different model of pricing and brand control—or at least a hybrid option.

The core issue facing many programs was that while brands loved many aspects of the affiliate network model, they found the technology overpriced as a stand-alone tracking solution for these direct partnerships. This was especially true for larger programs with considerable inbound demand to join their program. Additionally, after enjoying a near decade of 80 to 90 percent profit margins and limited competition in an industry with high barriers to switching network providers, some affiliate networks weren't very motivated to innovate their technology platforms. The result was that frequently requested technology improvements, such as control over invalid coupons or other changes that threatened the performance fee structure, always seemed to be on a future "road map." This inaction opened the door for a new class of technology-driven competitors to enter the partnership space. Once these competitors arrived, the full potential of marketing partnership automation began to take shape.

Technological Acceleration

The solution to many of the limitations described above came from the rise of software-as-a-service (SaaS) platforms. These platforms offer the same basic functionality as an affiliate network with two key differentiators. First, the software is licensed under a private label model, removing the need for cobranding and allowing brands to have more control of their programs. Second, SaaS platforms initially offered a pricing model that better aligned with advertisers' needs and objectives, especially for entrenched programs in the most established markets. SaaS platforms are often, but not exclusively, priced based on data usage rather than a percentage of sales or commissions paid. In these cases, your costs as a percentage of sales decrease as you grow revenue on the platform.

These SaaS platforms were developed in direct response to some of the known pain points of affiliate networks for enterprise brands. Two of the first and largest SaaS platforms, Impact

Radius, now Impact, and Performance Horizon Group, now Partnerize, were started by former leaders of affiliate networks at around the same time. Recognizing the ways that many networks had grown complacent, these industry veterans seized an opportunity for disruption.

SaaS platforms offered the technology of an affiliate network but with a pricing and branding model that opened the door to new opportunities. Instead of offering managed services, the model was more similar to other digital marketing channels such as search, social, and marketing automation, where the channel's technology platform and the management of that channel were separate offerings from different vendors. SaaS platforms wanted to be valued as tech companies—a SaaS-based technology company can attract a much higher valuation from acquirers or investors than even the most well-run or profitable services firm.

As you might expect, these SaaS platforms launched by aggressively targeting the customers that could benefit most from their value proposition: large, well-known brands that were paying hefty performance fees for a concentrated group of non-proprietary, long-term affiliate partners. Many brands earned 80 to 90 percent of their program revenue from only a handful of their partners and were even managing some of those partnerships directly. Under the prevailing affiliate network fee model, this small group of publishers accounted for 90 percent of their performance fees paid to networks.

The SaaS companies' beachhead strategy in the mid-2010s, which was primarily launched in the United States, was targeted at moving this small group of mature, outsized partners to a SaaS platform. This migration often saved brands significant money with minimal effort. Several networks responded to this disruption by lowering their own prices considerably to keep customers from switching providers without making any real changes to their underlying offering or level of service. In any industry, suddenly dropping the price for the same product or service usually leaves customers feeling that they have been overcharged previously.

While many companies were initially drawn to SaaS platforms for cost savings, only a few initially realized how the platforms might let them manage other partnerships in new ways without having to share their data or proprietary partners. Brands soon discovered they could use these same SaaS platforms for many other marketing, sales, or business development partnerships. In fact, a wide range of a company's revenue-driving partnerships could be tracked on a single platform—one that offered the same features and scalability as an affiliate network, only without the significant performance fee.

Upon making this realization, several companies began rebranding their affiliate programs as partnership programs—

e.g., the Acme Company Partnership Program—and considering where else they could use the same platform and the same program to scale additional types of partnerships across their organizations, replacing manual processes.

Automating the management of partnerships from other areas of an organization is one of the most significant changes to customer acquisition and business development since the creation of the internet itself. This represents a new wave of partnership automation that is beginning to spread across organizations, akin to early revolutions in sales automation and marketing automation that created entire new industries of software and services. Affiliate networks and SaaS platforms—which we refer to from here forward as **partnership automation platforms**—can change the way companies do business, and their models will continue to converge over time. Just as partnership automation platforms have evolved to add more network-like functionality, it's logical to assume that affiliate networks will respond to market demand by continuing to augment their own offerings with a more SaaS-oriented option and possibly even a hybrid solution.

In a partnership marketing program, partnership automation platforms are leveraged to track and pay a very wide range of a business's partners on a performance basis under one digital umbrella or a system of record. This is the future of partnership marketing.

The Big Tent of Partnership Marketing

We've now reached an interesting inflection point, as companies are figuring out how to use the partnership automation platforms at their disposal to build entirely new marketing channels for their brands. Partnership automation platforms enable companies to seamlessly manage a network of partners who are committed to driving the same business outcomes as the brands themselves.

If your business has a successful affiliate marketing program, you may have already seen the efficacy of this model. However, as we've discussed, while this technology was first applied to affiliate marketing, it can be harnessed in many other facets of marketing, sales, and business development as well:

▸ Your business can operate its **referral and ambassador programs** on a single partnership automation platform rather than tracking and paying these partners manually or through a niche program.

▸ The same applies to **PR and influencer marketing**. If your business works with influencers, you can manage many of those partnerships through your partnership automation platform, setting the desired outcomes and agreeing upon what payment is due in exchange for those outcomes. Many influencer-discovery platforms are rapidly integrating with partnership automation platforms as they see this trend unfold.

▸ These platforms can also work for **business development and channel partnerships**. If your business has a pipeline of potential business development partners—ones who can drive revenue but fall below the threshold where it makes sense to go through the business development deal—those partners can all be onboarded into a scalable partnership marketing program in minutes.

▸ You can even work with companies that act as agencies working with the Triopoly, but **on an outcome basis**. For example, there are several companies that have developed technologies for bidding on long-tail paid search keywords; the companies will pay for the advertisements with their own money in exchange for a commission once they drive a transaction. This arrangement does not replace your existing paid search team or agency; it can supplement it in an almost risk-free way. If we return to the investing analogy, it offers further diversification to your portfolio.

We will discuss exactly how your partnership marketing program can absorb all these verticals in chapter 8. But what's crucial to know is that the partnership automation technology that revolutionized affiliate marketing can provide the same level of transparency, brand control, and scalability to many other areas of business. Most brands can benefit from removing manual tracking and payment from their balance sheets as often as possible. Without the cost of manually managing a wide range of partner relationships, companies can add even small-potential marketing partnerships without creating excessive time and effort costs. Housing all your partnerships on one platform requires less overhead, produces more marketing data, and provides easier management and scale, and it is this transformative technology that is allowing brands to leverage partnership marketing in ways that were not conceivable even a few short years ago.

Key Takeaways

▶ Partnership marketing programs are enabled by partnership automation platforms that allow brands to manage large numbers of partnerships automatically.

▶ Affiliate networks and SaaS platforms are the predominant players in partnership automation technology, with each category offering different structures, pricing, and features. Choosing the correct partnership automation technology partner is a key first step in building a program.

▶ A modern partnership marketing program allows brands

to manage all their marketing partnerships in a single auto-mated, scalable technology platform.

Up Next

How brands can use partnership automation platforms to lever-age a rapidly expanding marketing channel.

7.

Building Marketplaces of Marketing

"The internet allows the small guy a global marketplace."

—NASSIM NICHOLAS TALEB

Having introduced the partnership automation technology that is transforming partnership marketing, we can now think about how this technology can be deployed to create scalable results, borrowing from a successful model of the last decade.

In the 2010s, technology allowed companies to scale very quickly in traditionally resource-heavy industries, such as on-demand transportation and vacation rentals, without needing capital to purchase the resources needed to run those businesses. To use two popular examples, Uber is one of the world's most popular transportation companies despite not owning any cars, and Airbnb is similarly dominant in the rental business despite not owning any vacation homes. What these companies have excelled at doing, rather than investing in vehicles and homes and renting those to users, is creating a scalable marketplace where supply and demand can connect. People looking to make money with their cars or their homes can connect with people willing to spend money on those same items. Simply creating this marketplace can be highly lucrative in itself: Uber reported over $13 billion in revenue in 2019 before the pandemic hit.[1]

While Uber and Airbnb are the most famous examples of this marketplace business model, several other digital service companies have emulated this approach. Task apps like Fiverr and TaskRabbit connect people willing to pay for manual tasks with people who are willing to do them. Upwork has created a successful marketplace for creative workers to sell their services to buyers, benefitting from the rise of the gig economy. These businesses' crucial role is maintaining the rules and standards that all participants in the marketplace must follow. A successful marketplace business creates rules that allow for transparency, growth, and ease of payments. This marketplace business model can form the basis of marketing's future, especially through partnership marketing. Here's how.

Marketing Test Drives

One of the clearest benefits of the marketplace model is the way brands can use it to have marketers do the most important legwork for them in driving sales. One example comes from a partnership between Valpak, a high-value direct mail marketer, and a global food delivery brand looking to attract small and medium-sized restaurants to join their client list.

Customer feedback indicated a desire for the brand to partner with these smaller restaurants, but these lower-yield restaurant deals were deemed too small for the brand's business development team. When Acceleration Partners worked with this client, we recommended that they test a campaign making an exclusive offer in a direct mail piece to owners of small and medium-sized restaurants. Our team onboarded Valpak onto a partnership automation platform and created tracking links and QR codes to print on every mailer.

The Acceleration Partners team, the client, and Valpak worked together to develop messaging and creative for a direct mail campaign involving an A/B creative test that was sent to 50,000 client-selected restaurants across the United States. This test performed so well that the client and team were eager to run another campaign. Since that initial test, the partnership with Valpak has continued to flourish, testing different audiences, including retargeting closed lost leads, targeting restaurants using other services, and tapping into Valpak's robust data house for their largest national campaign, targeting many small and medium-sized restaurants in the United States.

This is the impact of partnership marketing done well—when brands create an environment where partners can work for them, they can leave the actual work of converting customers and leads to the experts. Partnership marketing offers a safe way for brands to test new channels and campaigns without having to invest heavily up front in an in-house team or media costs.

Earlier, we illustrated the challenges brands face in a marketing landscape that is constantly gaining new, highly specialized channels. Maybe your brand mastered paid search through Google, but just as you mastered that channel, everyone started shifting to Snapchat. In a fast-moving, highly specialized marketing ecosystem, it is difficult to excel at everything. Plus, even if you have the resources to hire a massive marketing apparatus, it takes rare foresight and great timing to invest in staffing a new channel just as it reaches its potential.

One of the best ways to maximize returns on a new marketing channel is to partner with the people who already excel at it. Brands can jump-start their marketing by leveraging experts outside their company walls. A reality today is that many of the best marketers often aren't looking for full-time work; either they are hired guns who command market rate to run campaigns for multiple companies, or they have launched their own firms to service a portfolio of clients with their specialties. These are free agents who evolve faster than brands. While you might not be able to hire many of these experts directly, that doesn't mean you cannot leverage their talents.

Brands can consistently work with these marketing leaders through the marketplace model. Your business can benefit from doing for marketing what Uber has done successfully for ride-sharing: use your partnership program to build a marketplace of specialist partners who acquire potential customers from a variety of diversified channels on an outcome basis.

For example, let's say our friends at the fictional Acme Company want to get involved in content marketing in the UK, but they aren't ready or willing to invest in building a team there. Instead, they can work with local partners in the region through their partnership program. Those local partners understand the market and have harnessed specific technology or pricing models that would require time and resources for Acme to build on their own. And best of all, Acme can pay for it all based on the outcomes delivered.

On a CPA basis, Acme is probably paying their partners more than they'd spend doing everything in house at scale. However, Acme will still save money as they test the market because they won't need to spend to recruit, onboard, and train their own in-house subject matter experts. This arrangement creates the rare win-win: the partners get a premium for the expertise and systems they have created, and Acme can enter a new geographic market in a cost-effective way.

Because it's very easy to add new partners to a partnership automation platform, a business can experiment with different channels by testing certain partners and partnerships and seeing if they get results before expanding the budget significantly. Partnerships can become a form of research and development, without the up-front investment—you just need to set the conditions for the partnership.

Just as companies like Uber and Airbnb drastically disrupted their industries, the businesses that leverage partnership marketing in this way have the same opportunity to outpace their competitors through crowdsourcing in a way that is profitable, scalable, and sustainable.

A New Fat Pipe

In chapter 3, we dug into the power that Amazon, Facebook, and Google wield in the marketing world. One of the reasons these channels are so popular is that they offer the tools and scale to easily deploy large marketing budgets. As a result, they are often looked at by marketing leaders as "fat pipes," where large marketing budgets can be deployed quickly through a high level of automation.

For example, if a brand wants to put a lot of budget into a product launch, their first instinct might be to run large campaigns through paid search and paid social. The Triopoly are massive platforms with huge reaches, and they make it easy to invest money at scale. As a result, they become the default option for big budgets that need to be deployed quickly. As discussed earlier, they are also the favored destination of venture-backed companies that are flush with cash to spend.

No individual marketing partner can match the reach potential of Amazon, Facebook, or Google. However, a marketing program that leverages the marketplace model to gather a large number of partners on a scalable, automated software platform can start to close the gap without paying the auction-level prices the Triopoly giants charge. Plus, a partnership marketing program offers the additional benefit of generating traffic from a diversified set of sources rather than forcing brands to depend on a single tactic or platform.

Partnership marketing has the potential to become a new fat pipe, one where brands are paying for outcomes and not inputs. When all your partners, from a wide range of marketing channels, are on a single platform, it's much easier to manage them as an integrated channel.

Smart Partnerships

As we discuss the potential of brands building massive market-places of marketing under their partnership marketing umbrella, it's worth pausing to consider: Are there enough partners to go around? The short answer is yes.

As previously discussed, the early days of affiliate marketing were dominated by a large number of affiliates, primarily coupon sites and loyalty partners. Then, as we also covered in chapter 2, a generation of publishers evolved the model in the past fifteen years, led by sites such as CNN Underscored and *The Points Guy*. Now, marketing partners have gained a foothold in an increasing variety of media formats: podcasting, performance-driven social media, AI-assisted shopping, and chatbots, just to name a few.

Publishers are creative, entrepreneurial people who are always looking to monetize their content in new ways. They also range in size and scope from moonlighting mom bloggers to publicly traded companies. All a brand must do is attract these partners, create trusting, transparent partnerships with them, and pay them fairly for their efforts. In fact, an entire branch of service in the partnership marketing industry is called *publisher development*. This service is the equivalent of a sales team for partnerships; it helps companies build relationships with the right partners.

It's also worth noting that building a good reputation for

their partnership programs helps brands recruit and retain the best partners, creating a further competitive advantage in recruiting new partners. Programs have their own brand reputations, and partners prefer to work with programs and managers who have a reputation for integrity and reliability, separate from the brand's public or customer-facing brand.

In fact, we have seen over the years that many brands with great reputations among customers do not have the same reputation with their partners. It's critical to establish yourself as a great brand to partner with; otherwise, your recruiting and performance in the channel will suffer. There have been great brands that have fought an uphill battle in affiliate and partnership marketing due to the subpar reputation of their programs and management. By contrast, building a good reputation kicks off a virtuous cycle: the more the program matures, the more publishers it retains and attracts, which in turn provides better outcomes for everyone involved.

If your business doesn't have an affiliate program, the first step is probably to start looking into the available partnership automation technology.

If you do have an affiliate program, you might be starting to think about how you could expand it and incorporate other facets of marketing, business development, influencers, and channel partners under the partnership marketing umbrella. To do that, you will need to have stakeholders across your company better understand this model and become advocates (see chapter 10).

Key Takeaways

▶ Partnership automation technology allows brands to work with the best free agent marketers.

▶ Once brands have set up a marketplace in which partners can work for them and get paid for driving results, the risk and heavy lifting is shifted to the partners.

▶ The more a brand builds a positive reputation among partners, the better it will be at attracting and retaining partners. Partner recruitment is a virtuous cycle.

Up Next

A detailed guide to the many types of traditional and emerging marketing partners.

8.

Moving Your Programs to Outcomes—Who Are the Players?

"The hardest part about directing is getting everyone on the same page."

—ROB MARSHALL

We've spent the past chapters explaining why partnership marketing offers a valuable way to drive growth while diversifying your marketing portfolio. Now, we'll illustrate in detail whom you will be working with in partnership marketing and how you can apply the model's technology and payment structure to a wide breadth of marketing initiatives by consolidating them under the partnership marketing umbrella.

We'll start by introducing the partners that make up the partnership marketing channel, including the ones that have a long record of success in partnership marketing and the newcomers that are already showing considerable promise and gaining traction quickly. Then, we'll dig into the how: the tactics you can employ through these partners to build a scalable partnership marketing program you can leverage to launch new products, improve cash flow, and take advantage of a broader range of marketing partnerships.

Who Are Traditional Partners?

It's important to outline some of the most common players in the partnership marketing ecosystem, as these will often be tentpoles for your expanded partnership program. To clarify up front: any individual or organization that can drive performance based on outcomes you want can be a partner. However, there are specific categories of proven partners you'll want to know about to decide if they are right for your program. These categories can be divided into two camps: traditional partners and emerging partners.

Traditional partners are the ones that have operated on an outcome basis for years and represent the majority of publishers in a traditional affiliate program. While this isn't an exhaustive list, these are some of the main categories of traditional partners or publishers, with some representative examples.

- **Content partners:** These partners provide high-quality editorial coverage of a brand or product. They offer a great way for a business to introduce a new product into the marketplace, raise awareness, and get a gradual but steady influx of customers. These partners can require some time investment from a brand to ramp up and produce content that fits the company's message or focus. *Examples include Apartment Therapy and the Penny Hoarder.*

- **Coupon partners:** These partners target and convert discount-hunting buyers. They can often yield fast growth, as coupon sites typically cater to consumers who are already looking to buy a certain type of product and just need the right deal to push them toward a certain brand in that category. *Examples include RetailMeNot and Offers.com.*

- **Deal partners:** A deal partner operates similarly to a coupon partner, spotlighting specific discounted products to an audience of customers looking to buy. The crucial difference is that instead of offering a large collection of coupons at any given moment, a deal partner has a small number of featured deals to attract their full audience to a small number of products. A site that offers a Deal of the Day via email, for example, would be best described as a deal partner, not a coupon partner. *Examples are Brad's Deals and Slickdeals.*

▶ **Loyalty partners:** These partners offer rewards to customers who purchase from a brand, often providing cash back, loyalty points, or other incentives. Loyalty partners typically have audiences of savvy, avid buyers and are a good way to drive customer acquisition and retention. *Examples include Rakuten (formerly Ebates), TopCashback, and Giving Assistant.*

▶ **Subnetwork partners:** A subnetwork helps affiliates (content creators, bloggers, influencers, website owners, etc.) monetize their blogs, websites, social channels, etc. on a CPA basis. The subnetwork joins a brand's partnership program, brings a collection of existing partners to the program, and helps promote the brand to those partners. *Examples include BrandCycle and Skimlinks.*

▶ **Lead generation partners:** Rather than providing sales as their outcome, these partners generate qualified leads for your business in a variety of ways. Brands tend to pay these partners a fee for each qualified lead they generate rather than a percentage of a sale. Lead gen partnerships are most common in industries such as banking, insurance, and financial services, where transactions are often not closed in an e-commerce setting or there is an LTV beyond what is purchased in the initial sale. *Examples include Fluent and MaxBounty.*

An effective and mature partnership marketing program has several of these partner categories, each of which is handled differently and can be leveraged at different times, depending on the goals. For example, your business may want to leverage content partners to create interest in a new product, coupon partners to reignite fading demand for an older product, and lead generation partners to drive interest for higher-value products that a customer may want to purchase from your sales team directly rather than through a partner's recommendation alone.

Who Are Emerging Partners?

Emerging partners include the various channels your business likely already operates in, though most likely not with a partnership marketing framework and technology platform. While this is not an exhaustive list, these are a few of the best places to begin thinking about moving your marketing initiatives to a pay-for-outcomes framework.

BUSINESS DEVELOPMENT PARTNERSHIPS

Business development teams receive a significant volume of inquiries from potential partners looking to work with a brand. Many companies manage these partnerships manually, handling the contracting, tracking, and payment of these partnerships on an individualized basis. Business development partnerships typically require careful customization and negotiation, and they must be lucrative enough to warrant all that up-front work. Because of this, most businesses have a set threshold of revenue potential a prospective partnership has to offer them; otherwise, it is simply not worth the time. The bigger the company, the higher the threshold.

Once a business development team has set this threshold, any opportunities below that limit tend to get overlooked or outright rejected. You may recall this exact issue cropping up in the Valpak example in chapter 7—the delivery brand had the ability to partner with smaller restaurants but decided these deals were too small to be worth pursuing. This is where the scalability and standardization of a partnership marketing program can help. Because the cost and effort required to onboard a new partner to a partnership marketing program is low, thanks to the technology described in chapter 6, even smaller business development partnerships are worth pursuing in this manner.

While a medium-sized business development team may consider a partnership that will generate $25,000 a year in sales too small to manage on an individualized basis, adding ten $25,000 business development deals to your partnership marketing program and using a partnership automation platform to track and pay those partners adds up to meaningful revenue without requiring one-to-one management. These partnerships can also usually be set up in hours, not months.

If a brand has a partnership marketing program, its business development team no longer needs to decline potential partners that are considered too small. Instead, they can say, "we'd love to partner with you and can do so via our standard partnership program." These partners are added to the partnership automation platform the brand uses, and they are paid only for the outcomes they deliver for the brand.

A partnership marketing program can also serve as a proving ground for business development partnerships that a brand is interested in engaging with but simply does not have the team bandwidth to pursue. If a business development team is interested in working with a partner in the future but has to prioritize other initiatives first, they can add the prospect to their partnership marketing program to start cultivating the relationship. Then, when the partnership has matured and possibly even generated more revenue than projected, the business development team can revisit and see if more can be done or if more customization is required.

It's logical for business development teams to focus on the big fish. However, as Valpak proved to our friends the food delivery service brand, using automation to aggregate the smaller fish can create significant value with a lot less effort.

To execute this strategy and others that we will discuss, it's critical to create a good hand-off process and strong interteam coordination. If you are managing a partnership marketing program, get on the same page with your company's business development team to establish a process for sharing opportunities with each other to ensure that nothing slips through the cracks.

Begin by explaining how partnership automation technology allows your brand to facilitate partnerships with limited cost and effort rather than managing them on a manual, individualized basis. Then, ask the business development team to refer partnership opportunities that are below their threshold to you to consider adding to your partnership program.

When you're working across departments, politics always comes into play, so make sure your business development team sees this endeavor as complementary, not competitive. You're not trying to take partners from them; instead, you are simply finding a way to work with the partnership opportunities they don't have the time or interest to pursue. Also, a single platform doesn't have to mean a single budget or a single way of managing partners.

BRAND TO BRAND

Partnership marketing also provides major growth opportunities for brands to work together directly in the same customer acquisition workflow. While brands previously relied on simple cross-promotion campaigns, promoting each other's products on their sites or marketing channels, partnership marketing technology offers an automated way for businesses to drive customers to each other on an outcome basis with less effort and red tape.

A clear example comes from the travel industry. If you purchase tickets to a concert or sporting event in a certain city, you may be immediately prompted to click ads for flights or hotel bookings in that city. An airline brand such as Delta can partner directly with a ticket company such as StubHub, tracking the relationship through the partnership marketing platform without having to go through an expanded process with business development. These types of deals have happened for many years. However, partnership marketing technology now allows brands to build many of these business-to-business (B2B) partnerships on an automated, scalable platform, paying for performance and with the budget already approved.

We can expect these types of deals to occur more frequently in the future. As the process is automated, these types of marketing campaigns essentially become passive income—a brand gets sales through another brand's customer acquisition rather than needing to close all their sales themselves.

INFLUENCER MARKETING PARTNERSHIPS

From the earliest days of celebrity endorsements, many businesses have followed a proven model: popular, trusted, or beloved figures can persuade their fans to purchase the products and services they promote. As anyone with an Instagram account knows, this practice has exploded in the past ten years with the growth of social media–driven personal branding. Today, brands offer tons of free products and guaranteed fees to influencers in exchange for posts, reviews, and endorsements.

As is the case with many channels, this expansion in influencer popularity has also created a marketing apparatus to match. A large number of dedicated influencer networks have risen to connect influencers to potential brand advertisers.

Although the influencer channel has grown, it was certainly overfunded in its early stages, like many hot industries that attract a significant amount of capital. Because there wasn't enough business for the hundreds of networks that received venture funding, there are fewer players now.

The way brands partner with influencers has also changed significantly in several ways. More and more companies are looking for defined outcomes from their influencer marketing budgets. Companies are also looking for more authentic connections between influencers and the products they promote. The research firm Forrester found that, in the past few years, brands have been gravitating toward influencers who have smaller followings but have built authentic reputations with specific audiences.[1] These figures are often referred to as *micro-influencers*. For example, a cosmetics company may be more interested in marketing through fifty makeup YouTubers with small but loyal followings rather than paying top dollar to run a campaign with Kendall Jenner.

Brands also want to track these myriad micro-influencer campaigns similarly to how they track their overall marketing campaigns. At its core, the process of tracking, measuring, and paying influencers is really no different from the core process of a partnership marketing program. This is why brands are increasingly looking to integrate their influencer marketing channels into their partnership marketing programs going forward— effectively, they are already two branches of the same tree. Brands looking to build partnerships with micro-influencers are increasingly using their partnership marketing programs and technology to manage these relationships and pushing for more accountability through performance and hybrid-based fee models.

While you might be interested in paying a bunch of small- or medium-reach influencers up-front fees to showcase your product or brand, you can build these partnerships with less effort and financial risk by adding a large number of micro-influencers to your partnership program and paying a commission for each sale. Once brands learn to look past the star power of working with influencers who are household names, they find that micro-influencers provide a better ROI.

If your business already has an influencer marketing lead or team, use the same approach recommended above for a business development team. Small and medium-sized businesses don't have the bandwidth to manage hundreds of micro-influencers on a manual basis. You can ask your influencer team to refer those potential leads to you to consider adding to your partnership program. Plus, adding influencers to an automated partnership program is the most effective way to technologically integrate them into your marketing initiatives—automated tracking and payment are always better.

Influencer marketing has followed the same track as every other channel. Initially, it was sold through up-front fees and measured by metrics that didn't guarantee revenue. But many influencers are changing their approach, and measurability and accountability for outcomes are becoming much more common. This is the ideal time to bring influencer marketing into the partnerships fold.

MASS MEDIA PARTNERS

One of the selling points of partnership marketing is the way it allows brands to automate their partnerships with a large number of smaller publishers and content creators, turning many small fish into a massive haul over time. However, brands can also use partnership marketing for big-game hunting with mass media partners such as Yahoo (formerly Verizon Media), Gizmodo Media Group, and Vox Media. Just as we saw with Future PLC in chapter 2, these mass media organizations have discovered that marketing on a performance basis can be a foundational revenue stream.

Brands can use the outcome-based payment structure of partnership marketing to secure placements with even large media brands, generating significant exposure with a single article placement. The key to doing this is to follow the same principles of partnership marketing—transparency, communication, and relationship management—with even more care and nuance.

Of course, mass media partnerships have some unique characteristics that brands will need to know about up front. If you're facilitating a mass media partnership for your brand, it's important to set some key expectations in the beginning.

First, it's important to understand that these types of media placements often require significant time to develop. While a niche blogger might be ready to run a placement for a brand at a few days' notice, mass media partners require more lead time, more rigorous editorial standards, and more control over the relationships. There might also be a separation between the editorial team and the monetization team, and an editorial team may decide at the last minute not to run an article if they determine that it no longer fits their content strategy. Due to these factors, a mass media partner may want to make drastic adjustments to the brand's preferred messaging about the product.

Second, it is common for a mass media partner to require some kind of flat fee guarantee, depending on the level of exposure, though some are getting more comfortable with just receiving commissions, albeit at a preferred, higher rate.

Setting these expectations is crucial; you must be up front with any stakeholders about the wait time, editorial control, and the possibility of a deal falling apart at the last minute. However, if you clarify these potential pitfalls up front and protect your brand from financial risk, you can position your business to get a product featured in major publications and yield excellent ROI in the process.

PODCASTS

Podcast advertising is one of the fastest growing marketing channels, as the number of podcast creators and listeners increases significantly each year. In fact, Oberlo found that podcast advertising spending has grown from $105 million in 2015 to a projection of over $1 billion in 2021.[2] While early podcast advertisements followed similar strategies as television and radio ads—issuing a simple call to action to buy the product without providing a mechanism to track how many sales the ad actually produced—podcast advertising in recent years has been easily leveraged on an outcome basis, through special landing pages and tracking codes. For example, Tim Ferriss, who hosts one of the most popular podcasts in the world, with more than 700 million downloads to date, rarely does an advertisement that does not direct users to a specific landing page, such as www.acme .com/tim, or a vanity code "Tim" that can be tracked though to conversion. This same tracking method can be applied to any podcast partnership, allowing brands to measure the ROI of each podcast placement and prioritize the highest performance placements in future podcast marketing campaigns.

TECHNOLOGY PARTNERS

While technology partners have existed since the earlier days of affiliate marketing, new types of partners with different capabilities are emerging each year.

A technology partner offers a technological solution for acquiring leads or customers, increasing onsite conversion, increasing average order value, or providing one of any number of other value-added services under a pay-for-performance model. This broad category includes tools such as chatbots, automated calls to action, retargeting, tools that suggest complementary products or services, and even platforms that bid on long-tail paid search ads. You don't pay for the technology; you pay for the outcome, and these partners integrate as publishers through your partnership marketing program.

Many small and medium-sized businesses don't have the budget to test all these tools, but the model is not limited to just larger players. Rather than paying an up-front, flat licensing fee, companies can integrate with a tech tool and will only pay for the sales or leads the tool converts for them. It's a lower-risk option and creates aligned incentives. *Examples include UpSellit, RevLifter, and Increasingly.*

CHANNEL PARTNERS

Channel partners are another interesting group that increasingly fits under the partnership umbrella. These are distribution companies and resellers that specialize in selling other brands' products to their own base of customers or clients. In the past, these channel partners have been managed manually, particularly in a B2B context. However, managing these partners through a partnership program allows brands to use them in a business-to-consumer (B2C) context as well.

Sales through channel partners are often considered indirect sales because the transaction may not always happen through your company: channel partners often handle large portions of the process of selling your product to their client in exchange for a cut or commission of the sale. This might include going beyond the sale and supporting the end client directly. This strategy helps companies not only offset their customer acquisition costs but also decrease their customer support and onboarding costs as well.

Channel partners can include different types of businesses like resellers, service providers, agencies, and consultancies that provide complete solutions to their clients, from strategy to software selection and implementation.

Because of the sales cycle, rather than tracking the conversion in a shopping cart, brands often track sales through a CRM system, such as Salesforce, which requires different conversion tracking capabilities in the brand's partnership automation platform.

Establishing a channel partner program is especially important if you want to sell to larger enterprise businesses, which often purchase new software and solutions solely through their preferred channel partners.

Much like how affiliate partnerships allow you to scale your marketing function beyond your internal marketing team, channel partnerships allow you to scale sales dramatically without growing your team's headcount. Because channel partners sell and implement your product directly, they tend to require more education and resources than other types of partners during onboarding. However, you can still manage these partners under the same umbrella of your partnership program.

How, Not If

As is clear, one of the benefits of partnership marketing is the ability to recruit and work with a wide variety of partners. Once you've onboarded all these partners onto one tech platform, allowing you to automatically track and pay for their services, you can leverage these partners in varying combinations on any given marketing campaign.

Many brands make the mistake of dismissing a partner type or a specific partner out of hand without exploring the tactics they can use with that partner. For example, a brand may believe that coupon sites are off brand or that loyalty partners don't lead to incremental growth and new customers. However, blanket statements in this industry never hold true in all cases.

How you work with a partner is much more important than the partner itself. For example, a brand may rightfully not be excited about a coupon partner promoting a nonexistent code and inducing customers to click on it. However, they would be very happy to work with a coupon site on a campaign where the partner texts 20 million of their members or contacts them through a mobile app with a limited time offer that drives them to their closest store. Similarly, consider the benefits of a loyalty site that can build a lookalike audience based on a list of past customers and then target a lucrative cash-back offer to buyers who have never purchased from a brand's site before.

If you just broadly declare that you aren't interested in partnering with coupon or loyalty sites, you might not even know about these opportunities. This is why top partnership marketing experts are always in discussions with different partners and publishers to learn about their capabilities and custom programs.

When considering who to partner with, also be sure to remember that the technology in this space has come a long way. Your business can set up your partnership automation platform to automatically suppress commissions or to pay reduced commissions under certain circumstances. For example, if a customer bounces out of a cart and clicks on a coupon code site without redeeming an offer, you might lower or eliminate your commission for that type of situation. You can also pay more for new customers, limit coupon redemptions to valid offers, pay commissions based on volume or product category, and so much more.

The future of partnership marketing is about how, not if.

Brands can miss lucrative opportunities when they dismiss certain partner types without exploring all the nuanced ways they can work with those partners.

Key Takeaways

▶ Success in partnership marketing is about matching the right partners with the right tactics and campaigns.

▶ While traditional partners provide excellent value, emerging partners, such as business development, influencer marketing, podcasting, technology partners, and channel partners, offer even more growth potential in the channel.

▶ It's not a manner of if you work with certain types of partners—it's about how you work with them.

Up Next

A deep dive on key tactics and campaigns that can be executed with partnership marketing, with multiple real-world examples.

9.

Fill in the Blank with Partnership Marketing

"Why pay for marketing when you can instead pay for results?"

—VERNE HARNISH

Early in the COVID-19 pandemic, many brands expanded their budgets for partnership marketing channels such as affiliate marketing, enticed by the low-risk ROI and scalable results. While this was an especially natural shift for brands with experience in the channel, many more brands began to see the value of focusing more on tactics than on publisher types.

One of our clients was a luxury women's clothing brand that, like many other retailers, was struggling to move their products when in-person shopping had stopped entirely and even financially comfortable customers were wary of spending money on nonessentials as the economy tumbled. The brand was historically very resistant to the idea of partnering with coupon or deal sites to generate sales, worrying that offering any type of coupon or voucher would diminish their brand's reputation as a luxury good. However, our account team convinced them to give our proposed campaign a try, presenting it as a chance to turn inventory into cash at a time when liquidity was especially vital. The brand offered a 15 percent discount on many product lines during an eight-day period, working with many of the partner types referenced in the previous chapter, especially coupon and deal sites. The brand's partners required a minimum order value for buyers to apply the coupon, so shoppers felt compelled to add more items to their baskets to qualify for the discount. Our account team even worked with the partners to feature discounts on out-of-season luxury items, which the brand never imagined they could sell, especially during a very uncertain economic period.

To the surprise of even our team, sales of the discounted products increased by 24 percent during the coupon period—an unequivocal success. Broadcasting discounted prices during economic tumult allowed the brand to sell items they never expected to be able to sell and left the brand more than convinced of the efficacy of coupon partners under the right conditions.

As this company's story shows, even skeptical brands often come around on partnership marketing once they've seen specific applications and results. This is especially true when businesses realize that they can tie incentives to desired behaviors to meet a range of business objectives.

You're about to see the results partnership marketing can drive—the actionable tactics this model can unlock for brands, including case studies from brands that have gotten great outcomes in a variety of ways.

Launching a Product with Partnership Marketing

As all marketers know, raising awareness of a new product is one of the most important goals of marketing. While casting a wide net through paid search and paid social ads is a reasonable strategy for showcasing a product to as many people as possible, partnership marketing can provide a low-risk, high-ROI channel to promote a new product through partners with interested audiences.

For example, a brand might consider following the approach ButcherBox used, as described in chapter 1: reaching out to the influential content partners such as bloggers, podcasters, and product review sites in their market and asking them to feature the product on a performance basis. Making a strong first impression is crucial to an effective product launch, and your product gains credibility when a well-regarded content creator showcases it to an audience that trusts their recommendations.

In some cases, a partnership program can even capitalize on real-time events. In 2012, Michelle Obama was spotted wearing a ModCloth dress. As often occurred, her fashion choice was a subject of fascination in the media, and we saw an opportunity to help ModCloth capitalize on the trend. The same afternoon, in conjunction with the client's PR team, we released a marketing kit to every relevant content affiliate, giving them all the information about the dress they needed to craft their own posts about the dress with links to purchase. The kit was a huge success, generating hundreds of thousands of dollars in sales.

An additional benefit of product launch partnership campaigns is that a product recommendation can have real staying power after the launch itself. If a sneaker blogger recommends a brand's new shoe as a must-have, customers hunting for sneaker reviews will continue finding that recommendation months, even years, after the placement is first published. In some cases, a well-placed partnership marketing placement can generate long-term residual income for both the publisher and the brand, creating a long tail of revenue well after the product launches. This is the advantage of partners who rely on search terms rather than social posts. Social promotions have a much shorter half-life, whereas search terms can yield income much later.

Liquidating Merchandise Through Partnership Marketing

In addition to providing an effective way to consolidate and manage your marketing channels, partnership marketing can solve nonmarketing problems in your business as well. For example, it is a cost-effective, efficient way to liquidate aging inventory. Many retail businesses encounter inventory challenges at some point, such as when demand for a product drops or an economic slowdown occurs. Partnership marketing offers a solution for brands to convert old inventory into cash without having to pay up-front fees for digital ads or paid media.

Instead, brands can direct their partners—deal partners—to feature old or excess inventory items at a discount, alerting their audiences to deals. Many partnership marketing publishers you can add to your program specialize in showcasing discounts to cultivated audiences of bargain buyers. This approach is more cost effective and can often yield better results than a non-outcome-based ad buy. Plus, this tactic allows brands to move inventory without having to push a steep discount offer to their own customer lists or on the website itself.

We applied this tactic to great effect with a leading sportswear brand in the early weeks of the pandemic. As consumer confidence plummeted and companies needed to shore up their balance sheets in a hurry, we helped the retailer liquidate their excess products, including overstock in specific shoe sizes and styles. We partnered with several deal sites to promote deep discounts on those products in particular. The campaign started by offering a 50 percent discount, but partners could increase the discount rate if sales stagnated after a certain amount of time. The discount amounts and the timing of those discounts were agreed upon by the partners and brand in advance, and everyone was kept in the loop on any discount adjustments. The campaign worked—the discount offers jump-started stagnant sales and turned inventory into cash.

Plus, there's another benefit to liquidating inventory through partnerships: you can gather new customer information that you can use to connect directly with purchasers in the future. While a buyer may have purchased shoes from Nike before, Nike could get that customer's information only if they purchased from their website directly. Partners that drive customers directly to your brand's site are especially valuable for that reason.

Complex Commissioning

A decade ago, many programs would have had a default rack rate commission they applied to all customers. Today, in well-run programs, partners are paid different rates based on their value to the brand. This variation can be accomplished at an aggregate level with the specific partner, based on the tactic or by using smart commission strategies on an order-to-order basis. For example, you might choose to commission a coupon site at a higher rate for links used in an email promotion than for a link on their standard coupon page.

Smart managers today also leverage technology to commission the customer behavior or behaviors that they find most valuable. Here's a great example.

Recently, one of our clients, a clothing brand, was attempting to thread the needle between two payout systems: they wanted to increase commissions to partners who were able to acquire new customers for the brand, but they also wanted to promote steeply discounted offerings without paying too much commission for each item sold. The customizability of commission settings in the partnership automation platform is vital in situations like this. Our account team helped the brand work with the partners to reach a nuanced payment agreement: the partners were offered a higher payout above rack rate for each newly acquired customer, but the payout was lowered on discount and clearance items. This arrangement ensured that the company was not losing too much profit margin on their most steeply discounted items.

The program adjustment had an unexpected benefit. Because many of the brand's partners were able to carefully segment their audiences—separating their audience members who were already customers of the brand from those who were not—they were able to feature full-price products to potential new customers to maximize their own commissions while also driving higher profits and new customers to the brand. This is an example of how partnership marketing's variable pricing model can yield benefits for brands and partners.

The Rise of CPA

Once brands see how the CPA framework drives better profit-ability and alignment, you can expect to see it embraced more in other areas of marketing. This likely even includes paid search and paid social. One day, clicks may be viewed as having the same value that we consider impressions to have today. Google has hinted to some of its best advertisers that it is thinking about developing an outcome-based offering in the future. They obviously have the data capabilities to be a very strong outcome-based partner if and when they choose to go down that road.

Businesses would surely be willing to pay significantly more for each sale Google converts than they would pay for each click. While Google has no urgency to change their offering now, the growth in DTC and acquisition-oriented budgets might create more urgency for all the big players, including the Triopoly.

Partnership Pitfalls

While we are obviously big fans of the partnership marketing model, it would be disingenuous to present it as infallible. As with any channel, partnership marketing has strengths and weaknesses.

One of those weaknesses is closely connected to a strength: the potential for outsize returns. One of the great features of partnership marketing is that profitability is stable as the program scales, because revenue is always in a fixed ratio with marketing spend. However, this also means that partnership marketing will never deliver an unexpected home run, where conversions far exceed the cost of advertising. Partnership marketing does not drive stunning successes such as Dollar Shave Club's viral video, which, as described earlier, drove 12,000 customer acquisitions in two days.

As anyone who knows the stock market can tell you, investing in low-risk channels will protect your downside, but it can also limit your upside. While partnership marketing can reliably deliver strong results at low risk, those results by definition will not exceed expectations relative to the program's costs, unless the LTV of a given customer ends up being much higher than the company anticipated when setting commissions and payouts.

Also, the affiliate marketing industry had its fair share of fraud in its early days, which takes different forms in an outcome-oriented model. We discussed many of these tactics in more detail in chapter 3 of *Performance Partnerships*, and those experiences should serve as a warning to those leading partnership marketing programs today.

The main source of fraud in affiliate and partnership marketing is attribution fraud, where a partner earns a commission without adding any value in the transaction process. This is very different from the traditional click and impression fraud in other digital channels, which is targeted at the advertising inputs. For example, misattribution can occur through outright fraud from partners. Some partners did this in the early 2000s by using software downloads and browser extensions to manipulate click and referral data, giving credit to a publisher who was not actually involved in the transaction.

There are also several low-brow tactics designed to pull customers to engage with a partner after they are already in the buying process, even once they already have a brand's items in their cart. Partners can do this by creating phantom or expired coupons or by placing paid search ads on the company's trademark page, hoping to attract and convert customers who are looking to navigate directly to a brand's website.

As we discussed in chapter 6, the vast majority of these cases occur because of conflicts of interest and poor program management, which can be avoided by having the right oversight and team and by ensuring that the software does not provide commissions when these tactics are used.

A Vision of Partnership Marketing's Future

Throughout this book so far, we have explored how partnership marketing has evolved from traditional affiliate marketing into an effective way for brands to diversify their marketing portfolios and acquire customer volume at their preferred quality and price. However, for all the benefits of recent innovation, the partnership marketing channel is far from mature. In fact, it has significantly more growth potential when you consider how automation can scale business development through a vast network of partnerships. There are so many different types of partnerships that can be created—with different strategies, tactics, and economic models—that even companies with sophisticated partnership marketing programs can grow and evolve those programs. For example, the following are all likely developments in partnership marketing that we believe will come to fruition in some form over the next decade, listed in order of near-term to longer-term probability.

CONTINUED AGGREGATION OF HIGH-VALUE PARTNERS

Aggregation is nothing new in the affiliate and partnership marketing space, with companies such as BrandCycle and RewardStyle aggregating and managing publishers and influencers from the lifestyle and fashion verticals. This strategy simplifies relationships and processes for brands to access valuable partners through the existing affiliate marketing ecosystem and, in return, rewards the aggregators with a premium commission rate. As partnership marketing continues to evolve, we expect to see even more niche aggregation companies being created to drive highly targeted value for brands in a similar way.

A more recent example of aggregation is Showplace, which works with the top hosts on platforms like Airbnb and VRBO, creating contextual opportunities for brands to advertise to those hosts' guests and pay hosts a commission for each sale. As the publishing ecosystem expands, we expect to see more aggregation of high-value partner types in the near future, as many different groups seek additional monetization opportunities and begin seeing the value of partnership marketing.

OTT ADVERTISING ON PERFORMANCE

One of the biggest transformations in media today is the shift to over-the-top (OTT) platforms, such as Hulu, CBS All Access, and FuboTV, which are supported both by subscription fees and advertising. OTT is a means of providing television and film content directly to the individual consumer rather than having to go through an intermediary, which typically sells advertising locally in each market.

OTT advertising is attractive to brands because they can run targeted advertising that looks much more like digital marketing than traditional television ads. We appear to be getting closer to the day when clicking on content in a show and purchasing it will become a reality. When that happens, it's easy to imagine these services partnering with brands and offering ad placements on an outcome basis. For example, we could see the streaming service ESPN+ partnering with Dick's Sporting Goods to show digital ads for the jerseys of the teams of the sport they are watching, then allow customers to purchase products directly through the ad. In addition to serving ads in the correct context, this model would also make it clear which television ads were responsible for which sales.

"SUPER PARTNERS" TAKING MORE DIRECT CONTROL OF MARKETING ACTIVITIES

Today, most companies use a mixture of in-house and agency resources to manage their various marketing channels and must invest a significant amount of fixed cost toward that effort. Marketing is highly specialized today, and companies can occasionally fall into the trap of hiring several expensive experts for their in-house team or investing too much money in staffing one channel that ends up not being fruitful.

As we have already discussed, partnership marketing allows brands to avoid this pitfall by outsourcing parts of their marketing portfolio on a fully performance basis, reducing financial risk and offering a potentially better way to test new channels. However, we have yet to explore the evolution of this tactic by posing this question: What if a company could do *all* its marketing in this low-risk, outsourced way?

This approach has been pioneered by a fast-growing, somewhat under the radar company called Red Ventures (RV). RV has pioneered a model where it takes over entire marketing channels for its clients and is paid on a CPA basis, taking on the entire cost of marketing and even sales in some cases. Basically, RV goes directly to CEOs, asks them what a customer is worth to them, agrees to take on all the costs and risk (advertising costs, call centers, etc.), and delivers converted customers at that price.

While the majority of RV's clients are very large enterprises, smaller brands can embrace this same model through the partnership marketing ecosystem. It's easy to foresee an agency, or "super partner," that manages most or all of a brand's marketing channels on a CPA basis, then partners with experts in each of these areas who are also paid on an outcome basis. This creates full alignment for the brands, agencies, and partners and offers brands a comprehensive, lower-risk marketing strategy.

THE SUPER BOWL ON PERFORMANCE

This is the moon shot. Super Bowl ads are the pinnacle of advertising, giving brands a chance to reach an audience of upward of 100 million viewers. On top of that, Super Bowl commercials are an anticipated part of the event, promising brands a shot to introduce their product or brand to a global, captive audience.

At their core, Super Bowl ads have really been about branding and creativity, not performance. You may even have a hard time remembering what brand was behind your favorite Super Bowl ad. This approach is likely to create more scrutiny as budgets continue to move from brand marketing to acquisition. Here is a perfect example of this phenomenon in action: in February 2020, the streaming service Quibi bought a thirty-second Super Bowl ad spot, paying $5.5 million to announce its April product launch.[1] The ad might have made Quibi a household name, but not a well-understood one—a survey found that 70 percent of viewers who saw Quibi's Super Bowl ad thought the company was a food delivery service, not a streaming disruptor.[2]

Imagine paying $5.5 million dollars for an award-worthy ad only to learn that 70 percent of the audience did not know what you're selling. That's a failure, plain and simple, and not surprisingly, Quibi shut down in December 2020, less than a year after the big game.

Super Bowl ads make people laugh and chat about them at work the next day, but the cost doesn't always justify the return. However, what if, instead of being viewed as the ultimate branding opportunity, advertising at the Super Bowl was the ultimate outcome-driven advertising market? We see two ways this could happen through a partnership marketing framework.

First, it is entirely conceivable that a well-funded partner with strong creative and production capabilities, such as a loyalty publisher, could pay market rate for a sixty-second ad spot,[3] then create an advertisement with a very strong call to action for multiple companies in exchange for a performance fee or a base fee plus a commission. For advertisers, this is a no-lose situation; while some brands are wary of Super Bowl ad buys because it's nearly impossible to know the ROI, as Quibi learned, paying for this placement on an outcome basis limits the risk and provides brand exposure. And while the partner purchasing the ad placement is making a big bet that they can make a great ad that drives conversions, if the ad is a huge success, they might actually profit on the arbitrage.

The math on this adds up. Consider a case where a partner buys an ad for $5.5 million and asks for a premium commission of 20 percent to include an ad for a product—let's say, a new pair of sneakers—that cost $100. The partner would earn $20 per sale, so the brand only needs to sell 275,000 pairs for the partner to break even. In an audience of 100 million viewers, that means just 0.275 percent of viewers need to buy for the partner to recoup its investment. The brand, meanwhile, gets a big sales boost without the risk of a $5.5 million ad buy.

The second way this could work is for the broadcasting networks that host the Super Bowl—CBS, FOX, and NBC— to offer placements on a performance basis themselves, if they really believe in the product and the advertisement's ability to convert. Whereas Super Bowl ads have always been sold at a flat rate, if a network believes a brand has real upside potential and a clear, trackable call to action for the 100 million viewers, they may find it worthwhile to charge a lower flat rate plus a percentage commission of all sales produced by the ad. For example, if CBS could sell a thirty-second spot for $5.5 million, they may sell it for $2 million and 20 percent commission on each sale as a return of the advertisement or within a certain window. This means the advertising brand has less up-front risk, and CBS can take on that risk in exchange for a higher potential payout.

While Super Bowl ads are often valued for the prestige they give a brand, a popular ad doesn't guarantee commensurate revenue. This is a way to create measurable ROI and revenue generation, for both brands and partners, from one of the world's largest advertising events. It won't be long before Super Bowl ads move from giving super brand awareness to offering supercharged ROI.

Key Takeaways

- ► Partnership marketing can be deployed in several nontraditional areas, including product launches, liquidation, and more.
- ► Smart commissioning allows brands to set specific commission rates for their most effective partners and offer higher payouts for more valuable sales and conversions.
- ► We are still just beginning to unlock the full potential of partnership marketing—it has much more growth ahead.

Up Next

How to get the rest of your organization to join the partnership marketing revolution.

10.

Getting Company Buy-In

"If you dislike change, you're going
to dislike irrelevance even more."

—GENERAL ERIC SHINSEKI

As you have surely noticed, partnership marketing is a
relationship-driven channel and can require support and buy-
in from many different aspects of the business. To leverage this
model successfully, you need to get a lot of people rowing in the
same direction, including groups that aren't used to working
together.

Some of the people you need to get on board are obvious.
For example, as we discussed in chapter 8, if your company
has a business development team and you'd like to move some

business development partnership opportunities, you are going to need to get that team on board. However, you'll also need to earn buy-in for partnership marketing from other members of your organization, including leaders from outside marketing and sales, such as your finance team. You can't scale your business with partnership marketing if your colleagues slam the door on you. Here's how to pry the door open and keep it that way.

From Leaders to Believers

If you are the point person for the partnership marketing program at your company, you are going to have to demonstrate the channel's efficacy to get the budget and resources needed to grow it. If you have already operated a partnership marketing program, such as affiliate marketing, this task will be easier. However, it's possible that your VP or CMO, while familiar with the concept, hasn't actually executed it at your organization, especially in this form.

The first step is to understand what your company leadership wants. Every business wants more revenue, but your marketing leader may have specific goals or metrics they value in getting that revenue—high potential ROI, more leads, a certain volume of new customers, maximum return on ad spend, or something similar. Making sure you understand what your company leadership wants will help you identify how partnership marketing can meet those goals.

Next, demonstrate the effectiveness of the model. Clarify that once the program is up and running, the business has to pay only for the outcomes your marketing partners generate and that you can control and monitor both the quality of your partners and their performance. Although it may seem obvious at this point, you should stress and reiterate that *you are paying for marketing after you get the sale,* so any increases in spend or budget will mean higher levels of revenue, leads, or other corresponding outcomes.

Once you have established the basics, dig into the specifics of the model, including data on how the channel has grown and the case studies shared in this book. You should also outline the types of partners shared in the previous chapters and discuss how your business could work productively with each of them. The more specific you can be about what your brand's partnership marketing program will look like, the better. It may even be helpful to do some basic research on partnership automation technology and suggest a partnership automation platform that would best suit your company's needs. If you go this route, consider researching whether your competitors or industry leaders use partnership marketing and, if so, what platform(s) they use.

It's also useful to be up front about the additional buy-in you'll have to get across departments within the organization. If you can come into the conversation with your team's leader with a clear vision for the internal resources you'll need and how you can get those resources from other members of your organization—your tech team, your finance team, your sales team, and whoever else is needed—you'll have a better chance at convincing leadership to invest in your idea.

If this conversation goes well, make sure to agree with your manager on next steps. Be clear about what you will own in getting organizational buy-in and where you'll need your marketing leader to have your back when advocating for the channel.

Turning Scrooges into Big Spenders

Convincing your marketing leader that it's worth investing more in the partnership marketing channel is a good start. However, you must also persuade the guardians of the company checkbook, and that can be the toughest hurdle to clear for enterprising partnership marketers.

When it comes to championing partnership marketing, we always like to say that it's best to tell other stakeholders how partnership marketing can help *them* or even the organization as a whole. Discussing the efficacy and scalability of partnership marketing may speak volumes to marketing and sales teams but won't resonate as strongly with finance leaders. For finance leaders, the best thing you can emphasize is the ROI that partnership marketing presents.

When you're explaining the partnership marketing program to your finance team, start by emphasizing how partnership automation technology eliminates much of the manual labor of partner contracts, payments, tax forms, and other financial administration. This is a huge benefit for finance and something they might not realize. They will also appreciate that they don't have to carve out significant time in their schedules to execute payments for a partnership marketing program once it is up and running. You should also build some forecasts for finance, illustrating the volume and flow of revenue they can expect to see in relation to the commission payments that will be going out the door.

Discussing the economics of a partnership marketing program is crucial. It's helpful to divide the costs associated with the program into two categories:

- ▶ **Media costs:** The investment needed to pay commissions to partners.
- ▶ **Nonmedia costs:** The fixed and variable costs to build the technological infrastructure needed and to staff the channel going forward. This category includes any agency costs.

The more specifically you can estimate these costs, the better, as they are often treated and measured differently.

Remember that your leadership and finance teams are evaluating programs on an incremental basis. They're no longer taking partnership marketing or affiliate revenue at face value, because multiple marketing channels and partners within those channels can lead to a single transaction. Internal attribution models help define which channels are most deserving of the credit in different scenarios; you need to understand what your attribution model values most so you can align partners with those most desired outcomes.

Once you are done explaining the basics, you will need to really get to brass tacks. Your next ask is going to be the big one: a flexible and variable budget for the channel.

The finance department is often used to giving marketing a quarterly budget, which is then divided among a series of channels for the quarter. Each channel comes back with its data and makes the case for more or less money based on the previous cycle's results. This system causes a ton of horse trading as channels find themselves over or under budget within a quarter. Since some marketing teams can't get any more money in the middle of the quarter, they have to find a way to move funds between their various channels.

This strategy does not work well for partnership marketing for several reasons.

First, it's not a channel where you spend up front or can set a limit to your budget without constraining your results. Partners decide which campaigns they ultimately want to promote, and whether you end up under or over budget depends on how many outcomes your partners generate. Partnership marketing isn't as simple, financially, as setting a $1 million limit on a Facebook campaign and letting it run.

Second, if you are under budget, that's not necessarily a great thing. While it may mean your program was especially efficient, going under budget may also signify that you did not get the outcomes you were hoping for; when there is leftover budget, you likely haven't hit your revenue targets. Similarly, if you are over budget, that often means your program has exceeded your revenue projections. This is a good thing for a business—more money is coming in the door than expected. However, since many companies won't let teams spend beyond their budgets, this overrun could lead to some very awkward moments if the finance team doesn't understand the partnership channel.

Your finance team will naturally want to set a budget for the year. It is, however, critical that they understand that going over budget will also lead to higher top-line revenue, ultimately resulting in a better outcome for the business. This concept is well understood with sales commissions—no business would tell a salesperson to stop selling just because they've earned a certain commission volume.

The only way to get partners to stop driving commission-able sales—and using budget—is to tell them to stop promoting your brand or to cut their commissions. Neither of those solutions are recommended for the long-term health of a program.

We can't tell you how many times a brand has told us to set commissions to 0 percent during a strong quarter—usually the peak holiday shopping season—because their arbitrarily fixed budget has been exceeded. Doing this is akin to telling your sales team to stop selling because you didn't budget enough for commissions or, even worse, laying them off and asking them to return next quarter when budgets are reset. There is no faster way to damage a partnership program than setting commissions to 0 percent on short notice.

This move is also bad business. If you are happy to pay 10 percent for $1 million in revenue, you should still want to pay 10 percent for $10 million in revenue even though it costs you more in nominal dollars. Finance leaders are known for asking teams what they would do to grow the business if they had a higher budget, and a well-run partnership program provides an easy answer to that question. Very few companies cap their sales team commissions for this exact reason—it's always worth paying for profitable growth.

To be fair, you aren't actually asking your finance team for unlimited money. Instead, you are asking for the budget to be tied to the outcomes the program produces, not some arbitrary number. If you have the right quality controls in place and you are paying for marketing after you get revenue, there's no need to create an artificial cap. All that would do is put a limit on your company's profits.

Of course, asking your finance team to offer a variable budget will require a lot of trust. While the finance team might like the profit-and-loss aspects of partnership marketing, they have to ensure that they can monitor the program and plan for cash flow. Finance hates nothing more than big surprises; they like to predict accurately and mitigate risk.

This is where you need to commit to delivering frequent program reporting. Build a dashboard that provides weekly and monthly visibility into how the channel is trending and what the costs are for the quarter based on the progress to date. Keep finance in the loop on whether the program is running much hotter or colder than expected. Set them up with regularly generated custom reports from your partnership automation platform to ensure they have the information they need to feel good about the spending. As an added bonus, because you see the results of your partnerships in real time as sales come through, you can demonstrate the efficacy of the program more quickly.

You also need to carefully monitor each partner's performance and look for abnormalities. If someone is performing way above their average, dive in and make sure you understand why and that you feel comfortable about defending the request for more budget. The last thing you want is for finance to go out on a limb for you and be left with egg on their faces.

As a final persuasion tool, you can even tell your finance team they can pull back their budget if they are unpersuaded by the program's results as proven in the dashboard metrics. They will probably be happy with the outcomes once the program is up and running.

You won't have to sell your finance team if there are clear explanations of the costs of the program and the benefits it will yield. Let the positive outcomes for your business speak for themselves.

Getting Your Team's Buy-In

Let's say you are your team's marketing leader, and you're trying to pull together a partnership marketing program from your existing talent. Experienced talent is hard to find in the partnership marketing space, as we'll explore in the next chapter, so you'll likely need your team to divert some resources toward staffing the partner channel. This can be a tough sell, especially if you have a smaller organization.

Again, it's essential to showcase the benefits to your audience. While illustrating the revenue potential that partnership marketing offers your organization can be helpful, you're better off demonstrating for your team how partnership marketing can help them grow in their own careers. If they see the channel as a way to advance, your employees will be more excited.

First, emphasize that partnership marketing offers a chance for early career professionals to practice and showcase their strategic thinking. Launching a new program gives people the opportunity to set the strategic vision for a high-growth channel that can drive meaningful revenue for the organization. They can then use those results as justification for advancement, either within your organization or somewhere else, later in their careers.

Just as the brands that get in on partnership marketing early will benefit most as the channel grows, the marketing professionals who master the channel as it grows will reap similar rewards. There's a genuine lack of talent supply in the partnership marketing industry today, so there are plenty of opportunities for employees to become tomorrow's leaders.

Advocating for Partnership Marketing

The conversations explored above are the most common and pivotal ones for securing buy-in for partnership marketing across an organization. These strategies also lay the groundwork for advocating for partnership marketing in general, so let's revisit some of those key points:

▶ Partnership marketing is low risk and very focused on ROI. Brands don't have to pay partners up front, and they pay only a percentage of the outcomes they want, and only after those are achieved.

▶ A partnership marketing program that is running hot, or producing a higher-than-expected sales volume, will inevitably require more investment than you budgeted for initially. This, in and of itself, is not a reason to pull back budget. Because any additional budget is outgained by the sales the program yields, there's no risk in investing more than expected if the right quality controls are in place.

▶ Partnership marketing is built on transparency. While this book has delved into the transparency between brands and partners, that same degree of openness is required between a partnership marketing program leader and the rest of their organization. Use all the available data to make your case, both before you scale up your partnership program and while it is ongoing.

▸ Partnership marketing allows you to customize and optimize each partner relationship. You can ensure you are using the right partner for the right campaign, setting the proper commissions for each partner based on their previous results, and adjusting each partnership as necessary.

▸ Partnership marketing is growing, and that growth presents opportunities for employee development. Experienced partnership marketing professionals will find they are very in demand, both internally and externally, and they can use that experience and expertise to build their careers.

Using the strategies described above, you will be able to bring others into the fold and be viewed as a savvy, early adopter when partnership marketing inevitably becomes a vital part of your organization's success.

Key Takeaways

▸ Partnership marketing touches several areas of your organization and requires cross-departmental buy-in to be successful.

▸ Some leaders may be skeptical of partnership marketing, which is why it's crucial to emphasize its profitability, scalability, and transparency.

► Don't oversell partnership marketing. Instead, rely on the facts, set clear expectations up front, and provide consistent data to prove the program is working—and win your colleagues over.

Up Next

How to build the team you'll need to effectively execute a partnership marketing program.

11.

The Talent You Need

"One competent go-getter is worth One
Hundred incompetent do-nothings."

—KAILIN GOW

Let's say you've become convinced of the opportunity partnership marketing can offer your business, and you have
gotten buy-in from your CFO with your informed, data-driven
approach. Next, you have to figure out how to build your partnership marketing team.

It's common for companies—especially larger ones,
but also small and medium-sized businesses—to have their
partnership and marketing talent structured in silos or even
different divisions. Businesses typically also have business

development and PR teams that are siloed separately from the marketing team. Often, the first step in successfully staffing a partnership marketing program is having it seen as a channel and getting these separate teams working together productively.

A large company may struggle with the disconnection between its teams. A small or medium-sized business may not have the necessary level of talent at all. We'll talk about how you can either build the internal team you need to staff this channel or find external talent to manage it for you if you need help getting your partnership program off the ground.

Finding a Good Manager

The challenge of finding in-house talent dates back to the early days of affiliate marketing: finding one person to manage a partnership marketing program is difficult because the position requires several disparate, and often opposing, skill sets.

An effective partnership marketing manager needs the following:

- The ability to quickly build and nurture professional relationships based on trust.
- The skill set to recruit new partners into the program rather

than waiting for partners to approach them. The latter, passive approach yields inferior growth over time.

- The strategic aptitude to know what tactics to employ with which partners at which time.
- The technological expertise to understand the partnership automation technology necessary and to get partners onboarded into the right technology platform quickly and correctly.
- The analytical capability to evaluate program data, devise necessary changes, and convince others of the efficacy of those choices.
- The compliance acumen to set the rules for the program, ensure everyone is playing by those rules, root out sales misattribution and fraud, and hold partners accountable for those issues if they arise.

Even before partnership marketing expanded to include an array of emerging partners, it was difficult to find a single person who could do all these things well. Now, an effective partnership marketing team requires many of the skills listed above as well as expertise in a variety of channels.

On top of that, there is not a logical talent pool to draw from. Whereas a company can hire a Google-certified marketer to run their paid-search program, that same industry-standard verification program does not exist for affiliate or partnership marketing. While hiring someone with affiliate marketing experience can be a natural start—they understand the CPA model, the technology, and the relationship management needed to run a thriving partnership marketing program—even those employees are difficult to find and retain.

One reason for this is a simple misalignment of talent supply and demand. When affiliate networks dominated the partnership marketing landscape and were growing fast, they constantly trained new employees and brought new talent into the industry. The one limitation was that they were trained on a single platform and model. After a few years, many of the account managers from networks were often recruited away for in-house roles. Now, many of these affiliate networks are no longer growing at the same rate and therefore aren't recruiting and developing large classes of talent anymore.

But while supply has slowed, demand has only grown. SaaS platforms are growing fast, but because they aren't focused on developing account managers, there hasn't been a commensurate rise in the development of program management talent. Companies looking for experienced partnership marketing managers not only have a smaller pool to choose from but are also competing with increasingly more brands for that talent.

Another issue that has impacted the availability of

experienced talent is the industry's relatively short career ladder. For years, there just haven't been many roles above the title of senior manager in the affiliate or partner space. The only steadily available senior roles were on the executive teams at affiliate networks or agencies, and those roles are few and far between.

As a result, the industry has frequently watched its best and brightest move into other areas of digital marketing where there are more opportunities for leadership and growth. It has made more sense for a promising marketer to broaden their experience to paid search, paid social, PR, or other traditional marketing skills to open new doors and move into a director role rather than stay in the affiliate channel and get stuck at a manager level.

Because partnership marketing, as described in this book, is still an emerging channel even after twenty years, this same lack of advancement potential exists today. Many companies don't currently have roles such as VP of Partnerships, Senior Director of Partnership Marketing, or even Chief Partnerships Officer. When junior employees don't see these types of roles on the org chart or in their development path, they may be well justified to choose another course.

The industry needs to solve this problem before the talent well runs dry. When brands realize the revenue potential and ROI that partnership marketing offers, they will be compelled to invest in senior leadership roles in the channel and focus on retaining their talent. Partnership marketing certainly offers the growth potential to become a cornerstone of brands' marketing initiatives, and companies should capitalize on that potential by creating positions at the director, VP, and SVP level for partnerships. One can also imagine there being a need for a Chief Partnership Officer in some organizations fairly soon.

The companies that end up winning the talent war will do it by investing in recruiting the right talent to staff the partnership marketing channel, building a training program, providing a credible path to advancement for employees, and retaining them as they scale the channel for their organizations.

The Partner Staffing Playbook

As discussed previously, if you limit your talent search only to people with affiliate or partnership marketing experience, you'll have a difficult time staffing your program, as you will be fishing in a tiny pond.

The lack of experienced partnership marketing talent is a real obstacle to capitalizing on the promise of the channel. As an agency focused on recruiting this account management talent, we've certainly experienced the challenge of recruiting and training employees at scale to manage programs for our rapidly growing client base. However, over a decade of hiring, training, and promoting employees in the partnership marketing space, we've developed a playbook that can be used to build a great team.

The first thing to know is that premier partnership marketing talent can come from anywhere. For each of the essential partnership marketing management skills described in the list earlier in this chapter, there might be people at your company who have the skills to take on a specific role within the team.

▶ If you have a member of your marketing team or even your sales team who is excellent at finding partners and building relationships, they will likely excel at recruiting new partners to your program.

▶ A team member with data analysis and reporting skills can manage the data aspects of your partnership program. They can either allocate some time toward managing the data reports from your partnership program as it grows or do that full-time once your partnership marketing program reaches maturity.

▶ A member of your legal or accounting or analytics team who has an acumen for compliance and regulations might be good at helping to discover and manage fraud. While legal or accounting experience are by no means required for partnership program management, those auditing skill sets transfer well to compliance-oriented roles.

While some talent can be sourced internally, companies looking to build and scale a program will eventually find themselves looking for talent outside the company's walls. Often, a candidate does not need partnership marketing experience or even affiliate program experience to grow into a successful partnership marketing manager. This brings us to the first step of our partnership marketing talent playbook: **hire for aptitude**.

Due to the supply and demand imbalance mentioned above, people with significant industry experience are expensive. If you operate in a hot job market, they can also be very hard to retain. Instead of focusing on experience, look for signs of a candidate's ability and growth potential. These are some of the characteristics to look for in a partnership marketing manager:

▶ Did they excel in their role early and demonstrate a drive and ability to learn rapidly? If so, they have the potential to learn the partnership marketing model quickly and easily.

▶ Do they have a track record of building external partnerships, working in a sales role, or managing relationships? These skills suggest an aptitude for recruiting new partners and building effective relationships with them.

▶ Have they worked on or even led strategic marketing campaigns, especially ones with external stakeholders? This experience can indicate an ability to design effective campaigns and leverage the right partners to get the best results.

While inexperienced talent takes more up-front investment to train, we've found after more than a decade of hiring affiliate managers that high-aptitude employees within the industry usually outperform experienced employees in the long run. With the proper instruction, people who are talented and driven to prove themselves can pick up the nuances of partnership marketing faster than you'd expect.

This brings us to step two of the playbook: **train thoroughly**. When you have high-aptitude talent, it's essential to give them the training they need to execute a partnership marketing program.

We've successfully trained many partnership marketing managers who had digital marketing experience but no history of working in the partnerships channel. Our training process typically starts with giving new hires detailed case studies, then having them shadow one of our more experienced managers. They are also trained and certified in the networks and partnership automation platforms on which they will manage programs. We also send employees to industry conferences to learn, to begin developing their networks in the industry, and to meet with publishers. Once this foundation has been set, they start by working on the administrative tasks of an account, then grow into managing client accounts and eventually become account managers.

Of course, this is our experience as a company that hires seventy-five-plus people a year in just this one area. A company for whom partnership marketing is just one area of focus may need a different approach.

Companies that already have a partnership marketing program, or at least an affiliate program, should document as many of their processes as possible for future hires. For example, you need to have a written guide for effectively operating a program—how to recruit partners, how to investigate fraud, and how to use the company's preferred technology platform.

If you are attempting to build a partnership marketing program from scratch, you'll likely need outside training resources to get your team up to the level at which they need to perform. You'll definitely want your managers to be trained to manage the partnership automation platform(s) your program operates on, which is something other members of your marketing team probably don't have experience doing.

You can also pull together training resources for partnership marketing by drawing from your in-house expertise in related areas. For example, your business development team might share some best practices on outreach, and your other digital marketing channels can share best practices for campaign design.

Once you've gotten a partnership marketing program off the ground, it becomes easier to build a strong training program for new managers. If you're operating an in-house partnership marketing program, you will likely need to onboard only one person at a time rather than creating a training program to onboard entire classes of talent as we have at Acceleration Partners.

The crucial third step is to **create a career path** in partnership marketing. Few things stymie business growth more than talent turnover, and talent turnover often occurs when employees believe there is no path to advance within an organization. If you show high-aptitude talent how they can build a career in partnership program management at your company, they are more likely to stay for the long haul.

A key part of creating a career path is to promote people when they're ready for a step up. If your partnership marketing program is new and the most senior-level person managing that portfolio is a manager, it's good to plan for what it might look like for that person to reach the senior manager or director level, where they are managing people, not just managing a program. If a manager has mastered program operations, is scaling the program, and is ready to bring people onboard and manage them, promoting them to a senior manager or director role is a good way to reward them for their results.

Just as getting buy-in for partnership marketing in general

can take some effort, it may not be easy to advocate for promoting employees as soon as they are ready, especially if that requires creating a new position in the organization. However, if you don't find ways to keep your best talent growing, you will just be creating a revolving door for employees to quickly enter and exit your organization. You'll have a hard time retaining an effective partnership marketing team if there's no room to advance into senior roles. Remember that even if you are wary of creating a new role for your people to advance into, a competitor might be very willing to create that role and swipe your talent. This will become especially true once partnership marketing matures—and senior partnership marketing talent is in higher demand.

Once organizations have identified talent, trained a partnership marketing team, and scaled the program, the fourth step is to **consolidate channels** under your partnership marketing team. As previously discussed, there are a number of marketing initiatives that can be managed as part of a partnership program, including business development, influencer marketing, and mass media partnerships.

Once your program has matured, you really want to bring more and more aspects of your marketing under the big tent of partnership marketing so that it is viewed and managed as a single cohesive channel. And to do that properly, you need to have a strong leader who is able to set the strategy, manage the program itself, and then, eventually, lead and develop the team that manages the program.

The Role of an Agency

While the steps involved in building an in-house partnership marketing operation are not overly complex, most organizations simply don't have the in-house experience or resources to execute them properly without a steep learning curve. This is where working with an agency can be extremely valuable. A dedicated partnership marketing agency has the expertise, resources, and staff required to get a partnership program running quickly. They already have the necessary experience with the partnership automation platforms needed to build and scale a program, and they typically have a large existing Rolodex of partners who are a good match for the brand's products and campaigns.

An agency can work with a brand at any level of partnership program maturity and align it closely with the brand's interests. If you are launching a partnership marketing program for the first time, an agency can help you evaluate the partnership automation platform and supporting technologies needed and help launch and build the program, working with a lead on your team who oversees multiple channels. If you already have a program or a small team, an agency can serve as an extension of your in-house team, helping with aspects of the program operations or strategy that aren't in your team's wheelhouse. For example, if your team is focused on strategy and data analysis, an agency may help you with the crucial roles of program platform management and partner recruitment.

An agency can also provide the crucial service of taking a program global, which is the fastest growing segment of the market. A global agency has experience working with partners in a wide range of markets and should have account managers who speak multiple languages to cover a variety of countries. While operational elements of global programs can be centralized, a successful program must have resources in each market. For a variety of reasons, you cannot successfully manage an American program from France, or vice versa.

In addition, an agency can offer key expertise in the following crucial areas:

- Knowledge of all the partnership automation platforms, helping you narrow down the choices so you can make the best decision for your current and future needs.
- Proprietary technology and data for recruiting, onboarding, commission levels, and reporting, which can save significant time and resources.
- A wealth of experience in a variety of campaigns and the

ability to help your brand design a partnership marketing initiative for any given situation—liquidation, product
launches, special sales, and more.

▶ The capacity to maintain institutional knowledge on your
program. This is especially crucial for brands that have only
one or two people working on their partnership programs. In
these cases, a company can be seriously set back if one person
leaves and a new manager has to reestablish relationships with
all their partners. With an agency, turnover is less of a risk,
because the agency can ensure continuity of service regardless
of a company's staffing situation. Plus, larger and more experienced agencies should have multiple people working on
your program to ensure there is redundancy so that staffing
changes at the agency don't affect your program either.

▶ An agency can also advise your brand in dealing with partnership automation platforms and partners in your program.
If your business is navigating the dynamics of a partnership
program for the first time, it's useful to have an experienced
hand steering you through.

Also, crucially, working with an agency doesn't mean that
you are outsourcing your program. The idea of outsourced
program management (OPM), a term recently used with affiliate marketing, implies a diminished responsibility on the part

of brands. However, brands aren't turning the management of their programs entirely over to a third party and removing themselves from the process. Instead, they collaborate actively, both internally and externally, on the strategy, direction, and ideas for their programs. Our agency works closely with our clients, and we prefer to form genuine partnerships, with each partner doing what they do best.

Rather than an outsourced organization, an agency can be viewed as an extension of your team to help build your in-house program, allowing you to bring in global expansion, program expertise, and other capabilities. You always have the option to run your in-house program if and when it makes sense to do so.

Be warned, however, that finding the right partnership marketing agency isn't always easy. There are many agencies that misrepresent their partnership marketing experience; for example, we have frequently seen large holding companies, or agencies of record (AOR) that have been contracted to run large affiliate programs for brands but do not have the in-house talent to manage those programs. AORs often look to subcontract the work to other firms after they earn the broader account.

If you want to work with an agency, look for specialized firms that offer partnership marketing as a primary service rather than a service they list as one option on a huge menu to entice brands that are looking for one-stop shopping.

And if you hire an agency to work on your global program, make sure they have full-time employees in the market where your program will operate, not contractors or people working overseas and relying on Google Translate. Effective publisher development requires an in-market presence and local language capabilities.

With the right team, partnership marketing can yield fast revenue in the short term and scalability in the long run. Just as the channel itself requires some investment to yield significant returns, businesses will also need to invest in staffing the partnership marketing channel to reap the long-term benefits the industry offers.

This isn't easy, even if it's worthwhile. Working with an agency can help you kick-start your program until you are ready to staff it yourself, if that makes sense for your business. Again, it isn't outsourcing your program in a traditional sense—instead, it's more akin to hiring a contractor to build you a house. At the end of the day, it's still your home, not the contractor's.

As the leaders of an agency that sells partnership marketing services, we are aware of our bias on this subject. However, most brands need experienced help when starting a program from scratch or when someone inexperienced takes over the program; unsupervised, on-the-job learning is just too costly to attempt.

At least once a month, we are introduced to a new prospective or current client who is now in charge of the channel but does not have any affiliate or partnership marketing experience. Your business probably wouldn't hire someone with no experience to manage a $10 million paid search or social program, so why would this be okay with partnership marketing? If you're new to the channel, it's smart to ask for help and learn what you don't know.

Partnership marketing offers enormous potential, and having the right team is a huge part of the equation.

Key Takeaways

▶ Partnership marketing has suffered from a dearth of talent, though that will change as the channel grows.

▶ A perfect partnerships manager is nearly impossible to find. It's better to identify high-aptitude people and train them.

▶ You don't need to hire people with industry experience—in fact, you may have better luck looking outside the partnerships industry for candidates with high aptitude.

▶ Working with an agency is an effective way for brands to avoid having to staff the channel themselves.

Up Next

The final case for valuing outcomes.

Conclusion

The Final Case
for Valuing Outcomes

"Show me the incentive, and I
will show you the outcome."

—CHARLIE MUNGER

In September 2008, the American public realized they had placed too much trust in a precarious foundation: the housing market.

For the previous three decades, mortgage-backed securities, or mortgage bonds, were considered one of the most stable possible investments. Mortgage payments were considered the top financial priority for all homeowners, and most people believed that banks gave out loans judiciously, to financially solvent home buyers, to ensure an acceptable level of risk and a significant piece of collateral behind the loan.

As everyone now knows, this assumption became cat-
astrophically incorrect. The rules of the game had changed
behind the scenes. When housing prices collapsed, it almost
brought down the entire financial system, and the questions
began. Paramount among them was this: How did the American
housing market, considered one of the steadiest economic verticals, become so unstable that it ushered in a once-in-a-lifetime
economic crash?

The answer is surprisingly simple. Mortgage brokers' incentives changed, and their desired outcome and associated behaviors changed along with it.

This incentive shift was most drastically driven by the
popularization of collateralized debt obligations (CDOs)—
essentially bonds sold to investors with large collections of
mortgage loans serving as collateral.[1] CDOs allowed banks to
sell their mortgages and get paid well for doing so rather than
keeping the loans on their own books. Bankers were able to
bundle together enormous quantities of mortgages into CDOs,
then divide them into tranches that could be sold to investors at
a handsome profit. These tranches, in turn, were rated by risk-
assessment agencies that received significant money to give a
favorable rating to each tranche, regardless of its actual quality.
The better the ratings, the easier it was to sell loans to investors.

CDOs completely changed the mortgage lenders' approach.

Suddenly, rather than giving loans to qualified home buyers, banks were incentivized to give out as many mortgages as possible, then turn around and sell them to an investor who would create a CDO.

Lenders no longer needed income verification, good credit scores, or even substantial down payments from loan applicants. As a result, mortgages were given to millions of people who weren't in a financial position to actually pay for a home over time. The desired outcome was no longer to find safe and reliable borrowers; it was to issue and sell as many loans as possible.

The housing collapse was entirely inevitable in hindsight. Michael Lewis's *The Big Short* even shares a story of several financial operators who foresaw the crisis, bet against the housing market, and cleaned up in the process. But the people actually participating in the process had very strong incentives to keep the party going, leaving them blind to the risks.

In business, behavior almost always follows the available incentives. We see this regularly in sales. Business leaders often assume that creating incentives for salespeople is a consistently good way to drive results—salespeople who get commissions for every sale are motivated to sell as much as possible, driving revenue for the business.

But any experienced sales leader knows incentives are a double-edged sword; salespeople will often devote their sales strategies to maximizing their incentives, even if doing so isn't necessarily what's best for the company. They may push products with the highest commissions or try to overprice their accounts if they need to make quota. The best sales leaders know there is a delicate balance to creating incentives that serve their salespeople, the business, and the customers.

In many cases, incentives can drive a win-win outcome. However, incentives can also entrench existing behavior, stifle the rise of new solutions, or, in the case of the mortgage crisis, set devastating long-term consequences in motion for the sake of short-term gain.

Now ask yourself this question: How confident are you that the companies dominating the marketing channels you currently use are incentivized to drive results for your business? More specifically, how incentivized are Google, Facebook, and Amazon to focus on your ROI?

Hacking Incentives

Before the days of digital marketing, the reach of a medium—such as a television ad or a magazine placement—was the dominant metric, because it was the only way to measure performance. Digital marketing, in a similar vein, prioritized impressions and clicks as its currency in its early days and continues to leverage these metrics in places even after they have lost some value and relevance. While these metrics are often included in performance marketing campaigns, they represent the inputs an advertiser generates, not business outcomes that are guaranteed to drive revenue for brands.

Traditional digital marketing channels are filled with vendors who excel at generating impressions or clicks and prioritize delivering those results rather than helping brands generate sales or leads. Those vendors are incentivized to keep selling these metrics because they're easy to generate, and brands will pay for them. Business is good, and platforms don't need to change their offerings unless demand changes.

However, impressions aren't a metric that drives meaningful results. In fact, it's extremely rare for a banner ad that yields high impressions to actually drive clicks or sales. In 2013, Buzzfeed's VP of Agency Strategy, Jonathan Perelman, found that, based on the total available advertisement impressions and clicks, a person is more likely to summit Mount Everest than they are to click on a banner ad.[2]

As anyone who has ever idly scrolled through a website or social media feed knows, users constantly see ads without engaging with them or even processing what they are selling. Yet companies are continuing to spend heavily on this channel: an Insider Intelligence study found American brands will spend nearly $100 billion on programmatic display ads in 2022.[3]

Advertisers have successfully sold impressions for decades now, even if they don't always lead to the outcomes brands want. In fact, many advertisers didn't care whether the ads resonated with customers or were even visible to them. Some ad platforms have extensively leveraged pop-under ads, where an ad opens as a new window that displays underneath the browser window the prospective customer is using. These placements count as impressions for each site visitor, even if the viewer doesn't really see the ad.

Impressions are also the most easily manipulated marketing metric, but clicks can be just as misleading. Because Google knows they can always sell advertisement clicks to brands, they've developed excellent techniques to earn those clicks.

For example, there is a big difference between unbranded search advertisements and branded search advertisements. Let's say a sandals manufacturer named Mike's Sandals wants to start a paid search campaign. In some cases, a customer may buy from Mike's by searching "beach sandals" in Google and clicking on a paid link to Mike's Sandals. In other cases, a customer may visit Mike's site through an email campaign, decide they want to buy later, then search "Mike Sandals" and choose the paid link before the organic one. In both cases, it appears as though the paid link drove sales, but the reality is more nuanced.

As this example shows, it can be difficult to determine whether some digital ads are actually winning new potential customers or simply capitalizing on existing customer interest.

In any industry, it's safe to assume that someone selling you something has an incentive to sell it. They may not necessarily be selling you the product or service that is most effective for your business. This isn't because the salesperson is necessarily trying to rip you off or hiding better options. They are simply selling what their company pushes them to sell and may not even be aware that their product or service doesn't offer the best possible value to the customer.

The Triopoly doesn't have to offer guaranteed sales, leads, revenue, or even a certain volume of site traffic if brands are willing to pay for clicks and impressions instead. If marketing giants like Google and Facebook are financially incentivized to sell impressions and clicks, they'll sell them, just as mortgage brokers followed their incentives in selling to unqualified home buyers.

The problem is that while this status quo makes substantial money for the Triopoly, it often doesn't provide that same level of return for their customers. Many marketers have already seen this for themselves; they just haven't fully explored or discovered the alternatives.

It's time for businesses to start prioritizing channels that offer more transparency, better ROI, and more clear incentive alignments to create a diversified strategy. Partnership marketing offers the best way to accomplish that goal.

A Changing Game

This book has explored the changes in the business world that are dictating a subtle but considerable shift in how brands plan for and execute their marketing budgets. Companies today are selling direct more than ever before, exhausting their ability to exclusively market through the Triopoly, and facing increased threats from a privacy backlash, so they want to break the cycle of chasing the latest hot channel past the point of profitability. These brands are ready to begin building the foundation of a future that is more profitable and sustainable.

By now, we hope it is clear that partnership marketing is uniquely positioned to help brands excel in a shifting business landscape, all while ensuring incentive alignment between brands and their chosen marketing partners.

The purpose of this book is not to convince anyone to ditch their paid search, paid social, or retargeting campaigns. It's not suggesting that advertising through the Triopoly of Amazon, Facebook, and Google is always ineffective or will disappear, nor that these Goliaths will suddenly change their auction-style pricing model overnight. However, what can't be ignored is how quickly the advertising power in channels such as search, social, apps, and retargeting has shifted into the hands of a small group of big players. Many companies have too many eggs in a shrinking number of baskets, and that has left a real impact on profitability.

For years, Facebook has seen their average earnings from paid advertisements continue to rise. In chapter 3, you may recall us noting that the price of a Facebook ad increased by 47 percent year over year from 2020 to 2021. If you've run Facebook ads in the past several years, ask yourself: Did your return on ad spend ever grow this fast?

A case in point is the fast-growing consumer DTC brand Pela (www.pela.earth), whose mission is to create a waste-free future. Pela built its business on the Triopoly, focusing heavily on influencer and paid social media marketing, However, CEO Matt Bertulli put it best when he said recently, "the only thing that is predictable in my business is that my paid media costs will increase next year."[4]

Costs rising faster than profit is not a recipe for long-term success.

One of the most frequent questions we are asked by prospective clients, partners, and investors looking into the affiliate and partnership marketing industry is: How big is the market?

That question can be answered in a few ways. Historically, people have looked at a few well-known studies on the size of the affiliate marketing industry, which show that affiliate marketing is approximately a $12 billion annual industry globally and is growing each year.[5] Some more recent studies of the partnership marketing industry project a number that is double or triple that size to account for the expanded definition of partnerships facilitated through technology that we've explored throughout this book.

Even this projection may not be seeing the full picture, however. The real question to ponder is this: How do you estimate the size of a market that can potentially represent the digitization of an enormous percentage of business partnerships in the world today? How big is the market for business development globally? While we don't have an empirical answer, we do know that there's a massive opportunity to capitalize on this emerging market. It certainly starts with a T, not a B.

This is the real opportunity of partnership marketing and why the model will change the marketing landscape permanently. The impact will be similar to how Salesforce changed how companies sell at scale or how companies such as Marketo, Pardot, and HubSpot changed how companies market at scale. Those companies created the industries of sales and marketing automation that dominate the B2B landscape today. They've become so dominant that it's hard to conceive of how to build a modern sales and marketing operation without these platforms.

A similar level of innovation and automation is occurring with partnership marketing technology. These developments will completely change how companies think about, scale, and manage business development and partnerships going forward. The difference is that partnership marketing automation covers both B2B and B2C, making its potential even greater.

This change won't happen overnight, but it's happening faster than most people realize.

As more brands see the value of partnership marketing and eventually divert more time and budget to building robust partnership marketing programs, the Triopoly will notice. Supply and demand are undefeated, and even the largest companies need to respond to changing market forces. Even mammoth advertising platforms will be forced to adapt if their customers gravitate heavily toward marketing channels that are more outcome oriented.

This is a crucial moment in the marketing industry. Partnership marketing enabled by technology allows brands to build a scalable, profitable, sustainable, and integrated channel in verticals as diverse as affiliate marketing, business development, influencer marketing, channel marketing, and mass media placements. Businesses have an opportunity to shift away from marketing as it's always been done and finally align incentives and ROI in a way that would have been a pipe dream for marketing leaders only a few decades ago.

Don't be left wishing you'd exited the auction earlier or kicking yourself for seeing a new opportunity developing but failing to take advantage before your competitors did. Focus on the outcomes you want, find the partners that can deliver those outcomes, build your program on the right platform, and let the incentive alignment take care of the rest.

Notes

Introduction

1   Robert Kolker, "How NBC Universal Killed DailyCandy," *New York Magazine*, March 28, 2014, https://nymag.com/intelligencer/2014/03/how-nbcuniversal-killed-dailycandy.html.

Chapter One: The Case for Partnerships

1   Eric Budish, in discussion with the author, January 2021.

2   Pamela Bump, "20 Stats That Make the Case for Co-Marketing Today and in the Future," HubSpot, December 8, 2020, https://blog.hubspot.com/marketing/co-marketing-stats.

3   Deborah Bach, "From Farm to Cloud to Table, ButcherBox Serves Up a New Approach to Meat Delivery," Microsoft Transform, August 26, 2019, https://news.microsoft.com/transform/from-farm-to-cloud-to-table-butcherbox-serves-up-a-new-approach-to-meat-delivery/.

4   Mike Salguero, in discussion with the author, spring 2017, https://growjo.com/company/ButcherBox.

5   Meghan Grahm and Jennifer Elias, "How Google's $150 Billion Advertising Business Works," CNBC, May 18, 2021, https://www.cnbc.com/2021/05/18 /how-does-google-make-money-advertising-business-breakdown-.html.

Chapter Two: What Has Changed

1   *Encyclopedia Britannica Online*, s.v. "Barbie," accessed October 7, 2021, https:// www.britannica.com/topic/Barbie.

2   "Mattel Forecasts Holiday Season Growth as Toy Demand Surges," CNBC, October 22, 2020, https://www.cnbc.com/2020/10/22/mattel-forecasts -holiday-season-growth-as-toy-demand-surges.html.

3   Emily Glazer, "A David and Gillette Story," *Wall Street Journal*, April 12, 2012, https://www.wsj.com/articles/SB10001424052702303624004577338103789 934144.

4   "Affiliate Marketing Spending in the United States from 2010 to 2022," Statista, December 2018, https://www.statista.com/statistics/693438/affiliate -marketing-spending/.

5   "U.S. Ecommerce Sales (2011–2021)," Oberlo, accessed October 7, 2021, https://www.oberlo.com/statistics/us-ecommerce-sales.

6   Rosie Murphy, "Local Consumer Review Survey 2020," Brightlocal, December 9, 2020, https://www.brightlocal.com/research/local-consumer -review-survey/?SSAID=314743&SSCID=61k5_as5qq.

7   Robert Glazer, "The Points Guy on Affiliate Marketing, Partnerships, and Maximizing Travel," May 15, 2018, in *Outperform with Acceleration Partners*, podcast, transcript, https://www.accelerationpartners.com/wp-content/uploads /2018/07/Outperform_34_Brian-Kelly.pdf.

8   Sydney Ember, "New York Times Company Buys The Wirecutter," *New York Times*, October 24, 2016, https://www.nytimes.com/2016/10/25/business /media/new-york-times-company-buys-the-wirecutter.html.

9   Zillah Byng-Thorne, in discussion with the author, April 2021.

Chapter Three: Step Right Up: The World's Biggest Auction

1 Daniel Kahneman, *Thinking, Fast and Slow* (New York: Farrar, Straus, and Giroux, 2011), 292–93.

2 Ulrike Malmendier and Young Han Lee, "The Bidder's Curse," *American Economic Review* 101, no. 2 (April 2011): 749–87, https://doi.org/10.1257/aer.101.2.749.

3 Budish, discussion.

4 Greg Sterling, "Almost 70% of Digital Ad Spending Going to Google, Facebook, Amazon, Says Analyst Firm," MarTech, June 17, 2019, https://marketingland.com/almost-70-of-digital-ad-spending-going-to-google-facebook-amazon-says-analyst-firm-262565.

5 Jordan Novet and Salvador Rodriguez, "Facebook Beats Earnings Expectations, but Warns of Significant Growth Slowdown," CNBC, July 28, 2021, https://www.cnbc.com/2021/07/28/facebook-fb-earnings-q2-2021.html.

Chapter Four: Facing the Colossus

1 Stephanie Chevalier, "Worldwide Amazon Marketing Expenditure 2010–2020," Statista, July 7, 2021, https://www.statista.com/statistics/506535/amazon-marketing-spending/.

2 Emily Dayton, "Amazon Statistics You Should Know: Opportunities to Make the Most of America's Top Online Marketplace," Big Commerce, accessed October 7, 2021, https://www.bigcommerce.com/blog/amazon-statistics/.

3 Stephanie Chevalier, "Amazon Third-Party Seller Share 2007–2021," Statista, August 11, 2021, https://www.statista.com/statistics/259782/third-party-seller-share-of-amazon-platform/.

4 Jennifer Rankin, "Third-Party Sellers and Amazon: A Double-Edged Sword in e-Commerce," *Guardian*, June 23, 2015, https://www.theguardian.com/technology/2015/jun/23/amazon-marketplace-third-party-seller-faustian-pact.

Chapter Five: The Privacy Problem

1   Charles Duhigg, "How Companies Learn Your Secrets," *New York Times*, February 16, 2012, https://www.nytimes.com/2012/02/19/magazine/shopping-habits.html.

2   "Is Your Phone Listening In? Your Stories," BBC, October 30, 2021, https://www.bbc.com/news/technology-41802282.

3   Steven MacDonald, "GDPR for Marketing: The Definitive Guide for 2021," SuperOffice, May 4, 2021, https://www.superoffice.com/blog/gdpr-marketing/.

4   Carmelo Cennamo and D. Daniel Sokol, "Can the EU Regulate Platforms Without Stifling Innovation?," *Harvard Business Review*, March 1, 2021, https://hbr.org/2021/03/can-the-eu-regulate-platforms-without-stifling-innovation.

5   "California Consumer Privacy Act (CCPA)," Office of the Attorney General, California Department of Justice, accessed October 7, 2021, https://oag.ca.gov/privacy/ccpa.

6   Pamela Bump, "The Death of the Third-Party Cookie: What Marketers Need to Know About Google's 2022 Phase-Out," HubSpot, September 20, 2021, https://blog.hubspot.com/marketing/third-party-cookie-phase-out.

7   "13 Retargeting Ad Stats You Probably Didn't Know," Delhi School of Internet Marketing, accessed October 7, 2021, https://dsim.in/blog/2018/06/08/13-retargeting-ad-stats-probably-didnt-know/.

8   Seb Joseph, "Dire Predictions Aside, GDPR Didn't Kill Ad Retargeting (It's Growing)," Digiday, July 9, 2018, https://digiday.com/media/dire-predictions-aside-gdpr-didnt-kill-ad-retargeting-growing/.

Chapter Seven: Building Marketplaces of Marketing

1   "Uber Announces Results for Fourth Quarter and Full Year 2020," Uber, February 10, 2021, https://investor.uber.com/news-events/news/press-release

-details/2021/Uber-Announces-Results-for-Fourth-Quarter-and-Full-Year
-2020/default.aspx.

Chapter Eight: Moving Your Programs to Outcomes— Who Are the Players?

1   "Revlon's Cautionary Tale: The Changing Nature of Influencer Marketing,"
    Forbes, August 19, 2019, https://www.forbes.com/sites/forrester/2019
    /08/19/revlons-cautionary-tale-the-changing-nature-of-influencer-marketing
    /?sh=602495ee6dab.

2   Ying Lin, "10 Powerful Podcast Statistics You Need to Know in 2021," Oberlo,
    July 5, 2021, https://www.oberlo.com/blog/podcast-statistics.

Chapter Nine: Fill in the Blank with Partnership Marketing

1   Adam Epstein, "Quibi Knows You Have No Idea What Quibi Is," Quartz,
    February 14, 2020, https://qz.com/1795999/quibis-super-bowl-ad-launched
    -its-quest-to-be-understood/.

2   Benjamin Wallace, "Is Anyone Watching Quibi?," Vulture, July 6, 2020, https://
    www.vulture.com/2020/07/is-anyone-watching-quibi.html.

3   Brian Steinberg, "NBC Seeks Record $6 Million for Super Bowl
    Commercials," *Variety*, June 16, 2021, https://variety.com/2021/tv/news/super
    -bowl-commercials-price-record-1234998593/.

Conclusion: The Final Case for Valuing Outcomes

1   "What Is a Collateralized Debt Obligation?," Motley Fool, June 7, 2017, https://
    www.fool.com/knowledge-center/what-is-a-collateralized-debt-obligation.aspx.

2   Matthew Caines, "'You Are More Likely to Summit Mount Everest Than Click
    on a Banner Ad,'" *Guardian*, October 23, 2013, https://www.theguardian
    .com/media-network/media-network-blog/2013/oct/23/buzzfeed-jonathan
    -perelman-ad-banner.

3   Nicole Perrin, "US Programmatic Digital Display Advertising Outlook 2021," Insider Intelligence, January 11, 2021, https://www.emarketer.com/content/us-programmatic-digital-display-advertising-outlook-2021.

4   Matt Bertulli, in discussion with the author, June 2021.

5   "21 Affiliate Marketing Statistics," TrueList, May 3, 2021, https://truelist.co/blog/affiliate-marketing-statistics/.

Introduction

In 2017, our company, Acceleration Partners, made the decision to expand into the United Kingdom. One of the key decisions for our leadership team and our new managing director was how—and if—we could extend our remote working policy, which had existed for our American employees for over a decade and had become a foundation of our award-winning company culture, to the region.

At the time, working from home was even less common in the United Kingdom than it was in the United States, so our new managing director was understandably concerned that remote work would not be easily accepted by potential clients and employees.

Our experience with employees who worked remotely for

the first time when they joined our team was that they adjusted very quickly. However, we also understood the risks of entering a new market with a work style that went against traditional cultural norms. We ultimately reached a middle ground—securing a flex office space for our growing team to work together in person and to meet with prospective clients.

Then a funny thing happened. Within a few months, hardly anyone on the UK team was using the flex workspace. Even though remote work was new to all the employees in that region, they had all adapted quickly, and soon working from home had become their preference. Several of the UK team members enthusiastically communicated how much they appreciated being able to avoid their daily commute and shared that they could not see themselves ever returning to a full-time office environment.

Our global expansion experience illustrates what many companies have come to discover in their own remote work transitions. Some who have never experienced remote work wrongly assume it is untenable for their own organizations, and while remote work isn't for everyone, the reality—as many have come to learn—is that it's far more feasible than conventional wisdom might otherwise suggest.

Open Secret

For years, remote work has been gaining momentum, moving from a fringe business tactic to a model readily adopted both by employees and companies—even large, well-known organizations.

Even in the past decade, there has been a stigma surrounding remote work. People who hadn't experienced that workplace model pictured employees slacking off, lounging in their pajamas, and taking hours-long breaks throughout the workday.

Not only did this make prospective employees worry about working from home, it made clients and customers wary as well. Early in our company's history, we felt increased pressure to work exceptionally hard to prove we could deliver top-tier service even without an office. Some remote companies have even felt the need to hide their lack of an office from customers in order to appear more credible.

But times have changed, and this workplace model no longer needs to be a secret. Companies with remote work environments are more comfortable sharing the practice openly with clients and see it as an emerging competitive advantage to attract the best talent.

The United States has led the remote working revolution, with remote work growing by 44 percent in the past five years and 91 percent in the last ten.[1] However, the trend was beginning to catch on in other countries even before a global pandemic swept across the world in 2020 and forced nearly all companies to transition to remote work. And yet, despite having limited experience or preparation for that shift, a significant number of organizations found that for the most part, they were able to conduct business as usual. Many of their skeptical employees also found remote work far more agreeable than anticipated.

The Commuting Crunch

Long before the COVID-19 pandemic, the drawbacks of office life were becoming more apparent. The average American worker spent 225 hours, or nine days, commuting in 2019, and commute times have risen steadily over the past forty years.[2] The average commute in the United Kingdom is fifty-nine minutes *each way*.[3] In India, it's over two hours per day.[4] That's 7 percent of the entire day spent getting to and from work!

No matter where in the world people work, the commute keeps getting longer. This is especially true in areas where housing prices have continued to rise. In order to have an affordable place to call home, most workers have had to travel farther to get to work.

In most in-office organizations, the office environment doesn't help reduce stress and frustrations. The great open-plan workplace experiment of the past decade continues to be debunked from a productivity standpoint. One study by the *Guardian* found that employees in open-plan offices lose an average of eighty-six minutes per day to distractions, are 70 percent more likely than workers in traditional offices to take sick days, and are more likely to leave the office earlier in the day.[5] This adds up to a status quo where employees spend more time than ever commuting to work and get less done while they're there.

This is not a positive or productive trend, which is why when millions of workers around the world were abruptly forced to work remotely from home, most employees were far more open to it than their employers may have realized. Although COVID-19 triggered the largest remote work experiment in history, on a global scale, nonetheless, there's every reason to believe this new work-from-home reality will continue. Companies as large as Twitter have already told employees they never have to return to the office if they don't want to.[6] Moreover, I believe the organizations that can build a thriving culture in a remote workplace will be the leaders of tomorrow and will attract the best talent.

A Competitive Advantage

When I started Acceleration Partners in 2007, the decision to make our workforce 100 percent remote was initially an attempt to preemptively solve a pain point.

We are a specialized agency in a segment of digital marketing known as affiliate or partner marketing. In this model, brands partner with individuals or companies (referred to as affiliates, partners, and publishers) and pay them on a performance basis for delivering desired outcomes. It's an area of business that has grown considerably over the past decade but was more niche at the time, with small and diffuse pockets of talent.

We were winning large accounts and needed experienced account managers from the industry—talent that was scattered all over the country. There simply wasn't enough experienced and available affiliate program management talent in any single city. We assumed remote working would be a temporary solution, but we enjoyed the competitive advantage and flexibility it provided our company, as did our employees.

Building our team by hiring remote employees from across the United States allowed us to access a far larger talent pool than in-office organizations forced to hire within a geographic area. By committing to a remote strategy, we were able to hire the people we needed and offer them a flexible working style that increased retention and satisfaction.

This is an advantage that companies around the world can emulate, especially businesses that service clients or customers in multiple regions. As today's technology makes it possible for organizations in a wide variety of industries to operate with dispersed, remote employees, it's logical that companies around the world would use that capability to seek and acquire the best talent, irrespective of location.

For example, although our global expansion initially started in the UK, we leveraged our model to hire employees from across Europe to better service our clients in multiple countries. Those hires were easier and faster to onboard because we didn't need to first invest in an office in each market we serviced.

A More Even Playing Field

Hiring remote employees can also be an important step toward building more equitable workplaces. The reality is that the cost of living in cities such as New York, San Francisco, and London is prohibitive for many professionals, especially younger ones already saddled with student debt. The current norm of in-person offices in expensive hub cities tends to benefit those with more resources at their disposal. This presents a particular issue for people of color in the workforce, who often face economic disadvantages relative to their white counterparts. For example, in the United States, the average Black or Latino family owns under $7,000 in wealth, as compared to the $147,000 in wealth held by the average white family.[7] This wealth disparity manifests itself in more student debt, less access to higher-priced housing, and more dire consequences for taking entrepreneurial risks. When companies aren't limited to a talent pool in an expensive urban hub, it opens career opportunities for a wider range of people, regardless of their economic background.

While the ability to hire diverse pockets of talent is one great benefit of the remote work model, offering flexibility to employees is another crucial factor. The changing conversation and expectations around work-life flexibility continue to erode the appeal of a traditional, full-time office job.

There's been a global shift in how we talk about work-life integration. Increasingly, workers want more flexibility and autonomy; they want to be able to travel and have more personal and family time and even the freedom to launch their own side hustle. The rise of the gig economy has also increased job liquidity and expanded availability of contract work that isn't geographically dependent.

In the United States alone, there are six million more gig workers today than a decade ago. Three million of those people reflect the shift of the labor force toward this type of work and away from more traditional employment.[8]

These are talented people who might otherwise be looking for full-time work in areas where they would have fewer options available. They are also prospective employees who can simply opt out of the workforce, choosing instead to dictate how and when they work if the alternative is not attractive.

Organizations that offer remote work can excel by appealing to this exact group of people. If flexibility is becoming an increasingly desirable workplace trait, flexible and remote work is the best way to meet that need in a sustainable way.

Remote Works

One distinct advantage that organizations have today is that the remote model is more accepted than ever. Ten years ago, remote employees had to overcome the misperception that instead of productively working, they were focused on caring for their young children, watching television, running personal errands, or otherwise being unaccountable for their time and schedule.

It took years for remote organizations to overcome these external biases and prove they could deliver a high level of service without an office. The image in many people's heads of employees slacking off at home has been replaced by a track record of strong performance and results. The early adopters of remote work walked so the virtual businesses of today can run.

If you're considering joining a remote organization as an employee, starting a remote business as an entrepreneur, or making your team permanently remote, you're starting in a much better position than the organizations that came before you.

Creating a high-performance, remote work culture isn't easy, but organizations that commit to doing it with the proper foundation, playbook, and procedures can reap exponential benefits. I know this from our experience at Acceleration Partners. Since we decided to go all in on remote culture in 2011, we've grown over 1,000 percent in ten years and expanded our team to almost two hundred employees across eight countries. We have won multiple "best place to work" awards even though we don't have luxurious offices, Ping-Pong tables in the break room, or in-office baristas and masseuses. Clearly, these "perks" are not what makes a great culture, though in some cases, companies try to use these sorts of fringe benefits to cover up a poor work environment and encourage people to never leave the office.

Instead of prioritizing investments in a physical setting, we can focus on investing in our team members—personally and professionally. Because we are not interacting in person with one another on a daily basis, we excel by hiring people who value independence and flexibility, and we invest in their development from day one. That is a key skill set for the virtual working environment. We've even developed most of our own leaders—80 percent of people in leadership roles at Acceleration Partners have been promoted from within.

Remote work is the new frontier for the business world. I know from firsthand experience that remote work, when done effectively, drives greater happiness and engagement for employees and is a key competitive advantage.

Acknowledgments

First and foremost, to the incredible team at Acceleration Partners, who are constantly raising the bar and helping to lead the partnership marketing revolution.

This book had a lot of editors and a lot of eyes on it. Thanks to our leadership team, who contributed insightful edits and feedback to help us excel and improve. To David Rodnitzky, who read multiple drafts and provided important insight.

To Catherine Oliver, for her invaluable, thoughtful editing and input and to Mick Sloan, who put countless hours in carefully editing each draft.

To Richard Pine, Alexis Hurley, and the entire Inkwell Management team, for their ongoing support and partnership.

To our editor, Meg Gibbons, for supporting and fast-tracking this project. Also to Dominique Raccah, Liz Kelsch, Morgan Vogt, Kay Birkner, Kavita Wright, Erin McClary, and the entire Sourcebooks team.

Last, but not least, to our families, for their love, support, and patience as we've built Acceleration Partners over the past decade.

About the Authors

Robert Glazer

Robert Glazer is the Founder and Executive Chairman of global partnership marketing agency Acceleration Partners, one of the largest, longest-standing, and fully remote organizations in the world. A serial entrepreneur, Bob has a passion for helping individuals and organizations build their capacity to elevate.

Under his leadership, Acceleration Partners has received numerous industry and company culture awards, including Glassdoor's Employees' Choice Awards (two years in a row), Ad Age's Best Place to Work, Entrepreneur's Top Company

Culture (two years in a row), Great Place to Work and Fortune's Best Small and Medium Workplaces (three years in a row), and *Boston Globe*'s Top Workplaces (two years in a row). Bob was also named to Glassdoor's list of Top CEOs of Small and Medium Companies in the U.S. for two straight years, ranking as high as number two.

Each year, Bob's writing reaches over five million people around the globe who resonate with his topics, which range from performance marketing and entrepreneurship to company culture, capacity building, hiring, and leadership. Bob has been a columnist for Forbes, Inc., Thrive Global, and Entrepreneur and has also had his articles published in *Harvard Business Review, Fast Company, Success Magazine,* and more. As a speaker, he is sought after by companies and organizations worldwide on subjects related to business growth, culture, building capacity, and performance. He is the host of the Elevate Podcast, where he chats with CEOs, authors, thinkers, and top performers about the keys to achieving at a high level.

Bob also shares his ideas and leadership insights via Friday Forward, a popular weekly inspirational newsletter that reaches more than two hundred thousand individuals and business leaders across more than sixty countries.

Bob is the #1 *Wall Street Journal, USA Today,* and international bestselling author of four books: *Elevate, Friday Forward,*

How to Thrive in the Virtual Workplace, and *Performance Partnerships.* Outside work, Bob can likely be found skiing, cycling, reading, traveling, spending quality time with his family, or overseeing some sort of home renovation project.

Learn more about Bob at **robertglazer.com.**

Matt Wool

Matt is the CEO of Acceleration Partners. After joining the company in 2012 as its fourth employee, Matt served as General Manager and then President of the company before becoming CEO in 2021. During his tenure, Matt has been a driver of Acceleration Partners' success, including the company's numerous placements on the Inc. 500 list of fastest growing private companies, multiple Most Effective Agency nods from the Performance Marketing Awards, and numerous best place to work awards, including from Forbes and Glassdoor. Matt is a member of the Fast Company Executive Board and is a frequent speaker at performance marketing industry events. Matt lives in Western Massachusetts where he obsesses over his chickens and tries to ski as much as possible.

Resources & More

To learn more about the concepts, processes, and technology described in this book, we encourage you to explore our resources page, available at **accelerationpartners.com/outcomes**.

We are always interested in new ideas, partnerships, and feedback and would love to hear from you. Feel free to drop a line at **outcomes@accelerationpartners.com**.

About Our Company

Acceleration Partners is the premier global partnership marketing agency. By focusing on Better People, Better Processes, and Better Performance, our team sets the standard for how brands efficiently grow and refine their marketing partnerships anywhere in the world.

A trusted agency partner to leading brands, our team of seasoned marketers and industry experts help companies build meaningful, lasting, performance-based relationships with tens of thousands of partners around the world. Learn more at **accelerationpartners.com.**

Robert's Books

If you enjoyed this book, consider checking out Robert's #1 *Wall Street Journal* and *USA Today* bestseller, *How to Thrive in the Virtual Workplace,* and his first book on the partnership marketing industry, *Performance Partnerships.* Learn more at:

How to Thrive in the Virtual Workplace: robertglazer.com/thrive/

Performance Partnerships: performance-partnerships.com

Our Podcasts

THE ELEVATE PODCAST

Hear Robert's in-depth conversations with the world's top

CEOs, authors, thinkers, and performers on how to achieve better outcomes and business and life.

robertglazer.com/podcast

THE OUTPERFORM PODCAST

What exactly is partnership marketing, and how are the world's leading brands using this model to outperform in their marketing and business partnerships? The Outperform Podcast with Acceleration Partners shares insightful, valuable, and eye-opening discussions about what it truly means to create transparent, high-value partnerships that bring more customers, incremental sales, and faster growth.

accelerationpartners.com/resources/podcast

Please Leave a Review

If you got value out of *Moving to Outcomes*, we'd love if you could leave a rating or review on your favorite bookseller's website. This is the best way to help other people discover the book, so we appreciate all reviews: **robertglazer.com/review.**